SOUTH CAROLINA CIVILIANS IN
SHERMAN'S PATH

South Carolina Civilians in
SHERMAN'S PATH

Stories of Courage Amid Civil War Destruction

KAREN STOKES

Charleston · London

THE
History
PRESS

Published by The History Press
Charleston, SC 29403
www.historypress.net

Cover images: *Fleeing Before Sherman's Grand March*, from J.T.'s Trowbridge's *The South: A Tour of Its Battlefields and Ruined Cities, a Journey through the Desolated States, and Talks With the People* (Hartford, CT: L. Stebbins, 1866); *General Sherman's Entry into Columbia, Harper's Weekly*, April 1, 1865; *Columbia, S.C.—Sketched from the 17ᵗʰ Corps Front, Frank Leslie's Illustrated Newspaper*, April 8, 1865; map showing the line of march of Sherman's army through South Carolina in 1865, from William Gilmore Simms's *The History of South Carolina* (Columbia, SC: The State Company, 1922).

First published 2012

Manufactured in the United States

ISBN 978.1.60949.704.0

Library of Congress CIP data applied for.

Contents

Acknowledgements

The author wishes to thank the directors and staff of the South Carolina Historical Society in Charleston and the South Caroliniana Library in Columbia for their assistance and for allowing the use of their fine collections for this book. Special thanks to archivist MaryJo Fairchild, who was prompt and gracious in fulfilling image requests at SCHS. The advice and encouragement of knowledgeable friends and associates—in particular authors Mike Coker, Dr. James E. Kibler and Dr. Donald Livingston—were a great help to me as I worked on this project and pursued its publication.

Introduction

Much of what has been written about General William T. Sherman's march through the Carolinas focuses on its military aspects, but this book takes a different approach, examining the human toll, and it primarily presents the subject from the perspective of the civilians in South Carolina whose lives were affected by this campaign and by other military operations that followed shortly afterward. Many South Carolinians left compelling records of their experiences in letters, diaries, memoirs and newspaper accounts, much of which is corroborated by the testimony of Sherman's own officers and soldiers, as well as other eyewitnesses. During the fateful winter and spring of 1865, thousands of men and women, young and old, black and white, felt the impact of what General Sherman called "the hard hand of war." This is their story.

For four years, from 1861 to 1865, South Carolina was part of the Confederate States of America. Early in the War Between the States, Federal forces captured and occupied the Beaufort area on the coast, and the port of Charleston was blockaded by a fleet of warships. Later, Charleston was also subjected to a prolonged bombardment and attempted invasions, but in the state where the secession movement began, the last year of the war was by far the worst.

Of all the states in the Confederacy, South Carolina suffered the most under the army commanded by General William Tecumseh Sherman, and its troubles were not over when he and his soldiers were gone by March 1865. The following month, General E.E. Potter, who had already participated in

General William T. Sherman.

destructive raids on plantations near Charleston, led an expedition into the interior of the state under orders to destroy the railroad lines between Florence and Sumter, as well as to exhaust the food supplies in those areas. His force of about 2,500 men included five companies of U.S. Colored Troops (as they were officially called at the time), and his expedition, known as "Potter's Raid," was a continuation, albeit on a much smaller scale, of some of the destruction wrought by Sherman's army. Potter was still operating in South Carolina on the day in April 1865 that General Lee surrendered, but even the termination of the war that came soon afterward did not end further depredations in the state. Not long after Lee's surrender, Confederate president Jefferson Davis and his party were traveling through the state heading southward, and more Federal troops followed in pursuit, committing acts of pillage and violence wherever they went.

Shortly before General Sherman invaded South Carolina, he explicitly expressed his intention to ravage the state, writing to his superior officer General Henry W. Halleck, "We are not only fighting hostile armies, but a hostile people, and must make old and young, rich and poor, feel the hard hand of war…The truth is the whole army is burning with an insatiable desire to wreak vengeance upon South Carolina." In another message to Halleck dated December 13, 1864, Sherman reiterated that sentiment, writing, "The whole army is crazy to be turned loose in Carolina."

South Carolinians justly feared Sherman, knowing of his earlier destructive march through Georgia, where he had shelled Atlanta without notice, deliberately aiming his guns over the Confederate lines of defense and targeting the residential and business areas of the city, killing civilians there. Mrs. Robert Campbell of Bolton, Georgia, who fled her home to take refuge in Atlanta, recalled that during the shelling in 1864 "a shell killed a newborn baby and its mother in a house adjoining mine. I hastened into a bomb-proof, as fast as possible. As I entered the door to this shelter a sixty-pounder fell almost at my feet. Suppose it had burst, where would I have been?"

David P. Conyngham, a New York newspaper correspondent traveling with Sherman's army, wrote:

> *There can be no denial of the assertion that the feeling among the troops was one of extreme bitterness towards the people of the State of South Carolina. It was freely expressed as the column hurried over the bridge at Sister's Ferry, eager to commence the punishment of "original secessionists." Threatening words were heard from soldiers who prided themselves on "conservatism in house-burning" while in Georgia, and officers openly confessed their fears that the coming campaign would be a wicked one. Just or unjust as this feeling was towards the country people of South Carolina, it was universal.*

Conyngham gave a specific example of the soldiers' vindictive attitude, describing the case of a plantation house they set on fire and plundered early in the march into South Carolina:

> *The soldiers were rushing off on every side with their pillage. An old lady and her two grandchildren were in the yard alarmed and helpless! The flames and smoke were shooting through the windows. The old lady rushed from one to another beseeching them at least to save her furniture. They only enjoyed the whole thing, including her distress.*

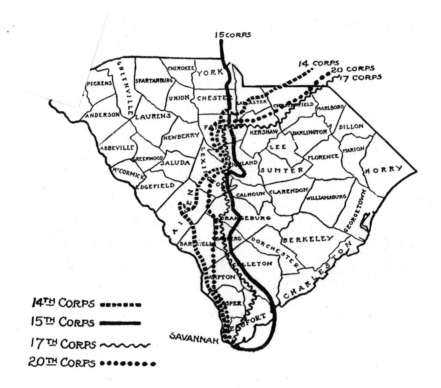

14ᵀᴴ CORPS ▪▪▪▪▪▪
15ᵀᴴ CORPS ▬▬▬▬
17ᵀᴴ CORPS ∿∿∿∿
20ᵀᴴ CORPS ●●●●●●●

Map of Sherman's march through South Carolina.

An editorial printed in the *Philadelphia Inquirer* cheered on Sherman's plan to wage war against defenseless noncombatants, rejoicing at "the fate of that accursed hotbed of treason." General Sherman himself regarded secessionists as traitors and wrote that the state "deserves all that seems in store for her." In a letter to Major R.M. Sawyer dated January 31, 1864, the general declared his belief that the war was the result of a "false political doctrine," namely, "that any and every people have a right to self-government." In the same letter (published in *The Rebellion Record* in 1865), Sherman contended that the Federal government could rightfully take the property, and even the life, of *anyone* who did not submit to its authority, and he complained that it was the "political nonsense of slave rights, State rights, freedom of conscience, freedom of press, and other such trash" that had "deluded the Southern people into war."

In January 1865, Sherman's forces gathered at Beaufort, South Carolina, and during that month a few of his brigades moved a little farther inland.

By the first of February, the main advance was underway. Divided into two wings, one under the command of General Oliver O. Howard, the army began to cut a wide path of destruction across South Carolina from the coast to the North Carolina border, burning farms, plantations and towns (including the capital city of Columbia); demolishing railroad lines; destroying or confiscating crops and livestock; and plundering and abusing civilians, reducing them to hopelessness and destitution. One of Sherman's aides, Captain George W. Pepper, recorded his memories of the march through South Carolina in his memoir, published in 1866:

> [H]*ouses were burned as they were found. Whenever a view could be had from high ground, black columns of smoke were seen rising here and there within a circuit of twenty or thirty miles. Solid built chimneys were the only relics of plantation houses after the fearful blast had swept by. The destruction of houses, barns, mills, &c., was almost universal. Families who remained at home, occasionally kept the roof over their heads.*

Sherman's armies met with little in the way of military opposition from the relatively small number of Confederate forces in the state, who were compelled to withdraw and burn bridges behind them as a force of more than sixty thousand Union troops relentlessly moved inland.

In 1865, Major George W. Nichols, an aide-de-camp to General Sherman, published a book about the campaign in Georgia and South Carolina, revealing his contempt for the people of South Carolina, whom he dehumanized as "the scum, the lower dregs of civilization. They are not Americans; they are merely South Carolinians." Nichols thought that the thievery committed against civilians (usually women and old men) by his soldiers was amusing. After describing how the soldiers would search out valuables that had been hidden away by civilians, he added, "These searches made one of the pleasant excitements of our march."

The soldiers sent out as foragers, usually in advance of the main army, were some of the worst offenders in terms of pillaging and other wrongdoing. These men were called "bummers." In his book *Merchant of Terror*, author John B. Walters described them as "brigands and desperadoes" who operated virtually free of any military discipline or restraint.

Of Sherman's accomplishments in South Carolina, Major Nichols went on proudly:

Sherman's foragers on a Georgia plantation.

History will in vain be searched for a parallel to the scathing and destructive effect of the invasion of the Carolinas. Aside from the destruction of military things, there were destructions overwhelming, overleaping the present generation...agriculture, commerce, cannot be revived in our day. Day by day our legions of armed men surged over the land, over a region forty miles wide, burning everything we could not take away. On every side, the head, center and rear of our columns might be traced by columns of smoke by day and the glare of flames by night. The burning hand of war pressed on these people, blasting, withering.

Another Federal officer, Major James A. Connolly, wrote home to his wife that halfway through the march in South Carolina, he was "perfectly sickened by the frightful devastation our army was spreading on every hand." He described the army's actions as "absolutely terrible" and reported how most houses were first plundered and then burned, and women, children and old men were turned out into the "mud and rain." He told his wife that he knew the campaign against South Carolina would be a terrible one before it began, but he had no idea "how frightful the reality would be."

John J. Hight, a chaplain of the Fifty-eighth Indiana Infantry Regiment, wrote in his diary, "Sometimes the world seemed on fire. We were almost stifled by smoke and flames." On March 7, 1865, Sherman's second in command, General O.O. Howard, wrote to another officer that "General Blair reports that every house on his line of march today was pillaged, trunks broken open, jewelry, silver &c, taken."

Historian Joseph T. Glatthaar, author of an award-winning book on Sherman's campaign in Georgia and the Carolinas, stated that the Federal army burned the capital city of Columbia (just as it had also torched a number of towns on its way to it) and that most of Sherman's soldiers admitted that they would do it. The Columbia correspondent for the *New York Herald* newspaper reported in an article submitted on June 21, 1865, "There can be but little doubt that the destruction of Columbia was the work of our army."

Arson and plundering were not the only outrages committed against the civilian population of South Carolina. Murders and other serious offenses also occurred. In her book on Sherman's march, historian Jacqueline G. Campbell wrote that African Americans, especially women, were often the victims of mistreatment by the Federal soldiers and that their officers were aware of these offenses. Black women, Campbell noted, were viewed by the white soldiers as "the legitimate prey of lust." During the time of Potter's Raid, a lady in the town of Summerton wrote of soldiers going after the young black women "every night," reporting that the girls had to hide in the woods to "save themselves from being ravished." During Sherman's march through South Carolina, Sergeant Arthur McCarty of the Seventy-eighth Ohio Regiment was found guilty of the rape of a girl who lived near Bennettsville, South Carolina. Several of his fellow Federal soldiers who were eyewitnesses on the scene testified against him at his court-martial in Goldsboro, North Carolina.

In addition to houses, crops, railroads and plantations, the irreplaceable public records of many South Carolina counties were destroyed by Sherman's soldiers. The courthouses of Chesterfield, Richland and Orangeburg Counties were burned, and the records of Beaufort and Colleton Counties, which had been sent to Columbia, were destroyed when that city was burned. Other counties that suffered significant loss of public records due to Federal vandalism included those of Barnwell, Horry, Lancaster, Lexington and Georgetown.

Many private libraries were also plundered or destroyed, as were a large number of important collections of great artistic, scientific and literary value,

Sherman's Fourteenth and Twentieth Corps crossing the Savannah River into South Carolina at Sister's Ferry.

such as those of Dr. Robert W. Gibbes of Columbia, Dr. John Bachman, the poet Paul H. Hayne of Charleston and many others.

In his travels with Sherman's army, reporter David P. Conyngham had seen much destruction in Georgia, but when he gave his general impression of the operations in South Carolina, he stressed how much worse it was than Georgia:

> *We marched, on the whole, four hundred and fifty miles, our wings extending some thirty-five or forty miles. This would give an area of over fifteen thousand square miles which we operated over, all the time supporting men and animals on the country. Indeed, the loss we inflicted on the enemy is incalculable, and all at a trifling sacrifice of life…*
>
> *As for the wholesale burning, pillage, devastation, committed in South Carolina, magnify all I have said of Georgia fifty fold, and then throw in an occasional murder, "just to bring an old, hard-fisted cuss to his senses," and you have a pretty good idea of the whole thing.*

Chapter 1

Destruction in the Lowcountry
and Midlands, January–February 1865

MCPHERSONVILLE IS DESTROYED

"There Was Left Standing the Presbyterian Church and Two Houses"

The village of McPhersonville was one of the first communities virtually wiped off the map by Sherman's forces as they moved out of Beaufort. Before the war, this village had been a summer resort for the planters of lower Prince William Parish in Beaufort District. Charles A. DeSaussure, who was born in McPhersonville in 1846, recalled in a memoir that the planters built themselves "summer homes—low, broad, wide houses, with large rooms and very broad piazzas…Each family lived in 'the big house' on the plantation in the winter and on the approach of warm weather, moved up to these pineland neighborhoods where they remained after the first or second 'Killing Frost,' when return was made to the plantation."

According to Francis M. Hutson, who wrote a history of McPhersonville, the village was deserted at the time Sherman's troops arrived. For part of the war, the inhabitants had been protected by a few Confederate troops in the area, including detachments from the Beaufort Artillery and General Wheeler's cavalry, but these were too small in number to defend the place against Sherman's massive army. Hutson recorded that McPhersonville was put to the torch in late January by troops of the Fifteenth Corps under the command of General John

The burning of McPhersonville.

A. Logan. "After the passing of the Fifteenth Corps," he wrote, "there was left standing the Presbyterian Church and two houses."

The church was the Stoney Creek Presbyterian Chapel, an offshoot of an earlier Presbyterian congregation established in the first half of the eighteenth century in the parish known as the Independent Church of Prince William's Parish but also called Stoney Creek. The earlier church, a frame building, was torn down by Sherman's soldiers, who used the lumber to build huts and possibly other structures.

CAPTAIN CROSSMAN'S DIARY

"Nearly Every House on Our Line of March Has Been Destroyed"

In early 1865, Norris Crossman, a captain in the Fifty-sixth New York Volunteer Infantry, was stationed near Coosawhatchie, South Carolina, a settlement located near the coast and the Georgia border. His regiment was under the command of Colonel Charles H. Van Wyck (later General Van Wyck). While General Sherman's army marched through South Carolina, the Fifty-sixth New York Volunteer Infantry marched north from Coosawhatchie up to Charleston, and Crossman kept a diary of his regiment's daily activities, which included the extensive destruction of civilian property.

The following are some excerpts from his unpublished diary of 1865:

Jan. 17—Coosawhatchie, S.C. Went out with a foraging party to Colonel Colcock's plantation on the Grahamville Road. Got considerable bacon, poultry, etc. and destroyed by fire some cotton, with cotton gins and other buildings.

Jan. 18—Col Van Wyck took about 200 men and went to Gillisonville with a detachment of men this forenoon. He captured three Rebels and a few horses, and some stores. Sherman's advance guard consisting of two squadrons of Cavalry arrived today. They have had no opposition while coming up from Savannah.

Jan. 19—Col. Van Wyck took about 200 men and went to Gillisonville. Maj. Smith and I went ahead and found the town all quiet. The Cavalry came up at 10 a.m. We secured provisions, furniture, etc., etc. The Court House and jail were burned, also the hotel, a store and two or three deserted dwellings. We returned to camp at 4 p.m. in a rain storm.

Feb. 21—On the march. Fell in at 11 a.m. and crossed the Edisto River… At Adams Run depot we found six rebel caissons partly destroyed by fire. The depot buildings was [sic] burned by our men. A great many houses have been burnt on our track today.

Feb. 22—On the march. Started at 10:30 a.m. and marched to Rantowles Station by 1 p.m. In the afternoon we went to Poplar Grove, the plantation of Tom Lowndes and there encamped…Buildings by the dozen have been burned today, in fact, nearly every house on our line of march has been destroyed.

Feb. 23—Poplar Grove, S.C. Maj. Smith with a party of 100 men went as far as the Ashley River and destroyed all the buildings along their route.

At Williams Middleton's place (Summerville) they found any quantity of clothing, etc.

Feb. 26—Fell in at 8:30 a.m. and marched to Charleston…We found the city pretty nearly deserted of white people. The lower end of the town is nearly destroyed by shell and fire.

GENERAL KILPATRICK BURNS BARNWELL

"Nothing in South Carolina Was Held Sacred"

Sherman's cavalry, under the command of General Hugh Judson Kilpatrick, entered the town of Barnwell during the first week of February 1865. The infantry troops who soon followed set up camp at the nearby plantation of Mrs. Alfred P. Aldrich, who reported in a memoir:

During that time their tents were pitched all around us, and our park lit up by their camp fires, and our yard and home filled with hundreds of rude soldiers…And so we lived for days and nights, with guns and bayonets flashing in our faces, and the coarse language of this mass of ruffians sounding in our ears.

One day a wretch who looked as if he had been brought from Sing Sing for the purpose of terrifying women and children, came to my piazza… carrying a rope in his hand, with which I learned afterwards he had three times hung up one of our servants, who had been reported to him as having aided me in hiding my silver…Each of the three times that this man suspended poor Frank in the air he would let him down and try to make him confess. Not knowing anything, of course he could not give the coveted information. Frank's neck remains twisted to this day. With this rope shaken in my face, the monster said:

"Madame, if you do not tell me in five minutes where your silver is buried I will set fire to your home!"

Fortunately, an officer who "repeatedly expressed his disapprobation of war, and his sorrow for what he saw going on around him" intervened and ordered the soldier to "let the lady alone." Her house was not burned,

General Judson Kilpatrick.

but she lamented that her "beautiful avenue of oaks had been ruthlessly cut down or killed by camp fires kindled at their roots."

Mrs. Aldrich remembered the sight of Barnwell in ruins after the army left:

All the public buildings were destroyed. The fine brick Courthouse, with most of the stores, laid level with the ground, and many private residences, with only the chimneys standing like grim sentinels; the Masonic Hall in ashes. I had always believed that the archives, jewels and sacred emblems of the Order were so reverenced by Masons everywhere…that those wearing the

"Blue" would guard the temple of their brothers in "Gray." Not so, however. Nothing in South Carolina was held sacred.

John J. Hight, a chaplain in Sherman's army, wrote of Barnwell in his diary: "Most of the business portion of the town, including the courthouse, is burned and other houses are burning continually...No effort was made to guard property, and the soldiers are permitted to take anything they desire."

The famous South Carolina author William Gilmore Simms asked, "On what plea was the picturesque village of Barnwell destroyed?" He continued:

> *We had no army there for its defense; no issue of strength in its neighborhood had excited the passions of its combatants. Yet it was plundered—every house—and nearly all burned to the ground; and this, too, where the town was occupied by women and children only. So, too, the fate of Blackville, Graham, Bamberg, Buford's Bridge, Lexington, &c., all hamlets of most modest character, where no resistance was offered—where no fighting took place—where there was no provocation of liquor even, and where the only exercise of heroism was at the expense of women, infancy, and feebleness.*

In his autobiography, Union general O.O. Howard recorded a conversation he had with General Kilpatrick during their march through South Carolina in which he commented on a "good joke" that he had heard, remarking to Kilpatrick, "General Sherman said you were changing the names of places about here, so that soon a new geography would have to be made. He said that he sent you up to Barnwell the other day, and that you had changed the name of the place to Burnwell." Howard noted that General Kilpatrick found this joke very amusing.

ELIZA ARMSTRONG'S STORY

"A Shameful Scene"

Sherman's forces arrived at Blackville, a railroad town in Barnwell County, on February 7, 1865. Eliza Armstrong was living here with her mother at the time, and in a letter dated February 21, 1865, she described their experiences:

The Twentieth Corps entering Blackville.

Words are inadequate to express our fright, when the Yankees first made their appearance in the village…Tuesday the 7ᵗʰ, in the morning about nine o'clock; it was an awful sight to see them rushing into the village by hundreds; I thought there would be no end of them.

Our men, Wheeler's Cavalry, were in the village; they drew up in a line of battle, stood nobly, and fired as long as they could, but the enemy rushed in such numbers, that, poor fellows, they were reluctantly compelled to retreat…

In a few moments we saw to our horror Mrs. W's house all in flames and the poor souls trying to save some of their effects; but it was useless…

Kilpatrick's cavalry stayed in the village from Tuesday morning at 8 o'clock until Wednesday afternoon, doing all the mischief they could, and they took care not to allow a guard until all the mischief was done; the guard we had stayed until every man had left the place, as there were always some stragglers left behind to do mischief, which the officers pretend not to allow when they are around.

Years later, Mrs. Armstrong wrote another letter to a Charleston newspaper in which she added "a few sketches which I can perfectly recollect" about her family's losses, as well as another incident that occurred in Blackville in which Federal officers intruded on a sick, helpless woman:

> We lost nearly everything we owned in this world…but the loss of personal effects was nothing to be compared with the loss of two lives, who were very dear to us. God alone knows our feelings when we received the terrible news that on Christmas morning of the year 1863, the lives of both my step-father, William Knighton, and Aunt Louisa had been swept away by the same cruel shells that were hurled into Charleston at that time…
>
> What I here state, I was an eyewitness to: a shameful scene. I had occasion to visit for a few moments a friend who was our next door neighbor, and who was sick in her bed at the time with her infant. As I neared her room (which was on the ground floor), I heard strange voices and on entering saw seven heathens, for not one in that group could call himself a gentleman. Four were standing by the fire and three were sitting on her bed, and she, poor creature, not able to protest in any way.

The Federal forces destroyed more than forty major structures in Blackville, including the railroad depot and everything connected with it.

According to an official report submitted by the assistant inspector general of the Confederate army, Mrs. Armstrong's stepfather, William Knighton, residing at the corner of Meeting and Market Streets, had his right leg taken off during the shelling of Charleston and died four days later. There were four other civilian deaths in the city due to the Federal shelling on December 25, 1863, which also caused a major fire.

Murder in Aiken

"James Courtney Slowly Bled to Death"

On February 11, 1865, the town of Aiken, located not far from the Georgia border, was the site of a battle that was one of the last Southern victories of the war. Here Confederate general Joseph Wheeler defeated

Federal cavalry under the command of Hugh Judson Kilpatrick, one of Sherman's generals. General Kilpatrick's men were forced to retreat, and Aiken was spared the destruction meted out to so many other places in the state. This Confederate victory also protected important military stores at nearby Augusta, Georgia, as well as the Graniteville cotton mill and a paper mill.

General Robert E. Lee called General Joseph Wheeler "one of the two ablest cavalry officers which the war developed." Nicknamed "Fighting Joe," Wheeler commanded in numerous battles during the war, was wounded three times and had sixteen horses shot from under him. A native of Georgia, Wheeler harassed the flank of General Sherman's army during the march to Atlanta and in August 1864 led a successful raid against that army as far north as the Kentucky state line. He was commissioned a lieutenant general in February 1865 and commanded the cavalry of General Johnston's army until the war's end.

James Courtney, a fifty-four-year-old civilian who lived near Aiken, was killed by Union troops while trying to save his house. The *Aiken Press*, a local newspaper, later recounted his story:

> *As Kilpatrick's men moved towards Aiken, residents of the county realized that their worst fears were coming true…Mr. James Courtney determinedly extinguished three fires that the Union Cavalry had started to destroy his home. Each time Courtney extinguished the fire, the cavalry would restart it. After the third time, the cavalry shot him in the leg to prevent him from saving his house. Mr. Courtney sent a request for a Union surgeon to come stop the flow of blood, but the surgeon refused to come. James Courtney slowly bled to death while his home burned in front of him. Courtney, possibly, was the first casualty of Aiken County.*

In his book about Sherman's march, Burke Davis wrote that some of General Wheeler's soldiers who were pursuing the retreating Federal soldiers near Aiken stopped at the house of a Baptist minister who was leaning on the gatepost of his farm, sobbing. The man told them that Yankee soldiers had raped his daughter and had just left. Wheeler's men immediately rode off in pursuit, caught up with the perpetrators and killed all but one of them, a wounded boy who swore that he had nothing to do with the crime.

DESTRUCTION AT OTRANTO PLANTATION

"You Are Now Suffering for What You Have Done"

Otranto Plantation in St. James Goose Creek Parish (part of modern Berkeley County) was the property of Philip Johnstone Porcher Sr. The house, which still exists, was probably built in the late eighteenth century.

In February 1865, Otranto was the scene of an enemy invasion. While Mr. Porcher (an elderly man) was away serving in the home guard, his wife, Louise, two daughters and two aunts were living at the house with a number of family servants. One of Porcher's daughters (Marion J. Porcher Ford) chronicled what happened in letters written to family members soon after the events. After mournfully watching the evacuating army of Confederate general Hardee passing by on the state road, the women busied themselves "secreting provisions and burying valuables" in expectation of the arrival of Federal forces in their area.

On February 22, two days after the last of the retreating Confederate forces were seen, the first enemy soldiers appeared at Otranto. Marion wrote:

> *The first comer Lieut. R. was very insolent. He smirked, sneered and jeered. His first question was, "Where's the man of the house?" We answered, "He is not here." He then said, "In the rebel army I suppose." We answered nothing...He seemed unwilling to leave and said, "I suppose you have never seen black troops. You will soon have that pleasure as they are coming up now." Mamma answered, "I am accustomed to negroes and never have feared them. Negroes have always behaved well to me." We now saw [them] advancing up the avenue...they were headed by a little officer (white) Lieut. J., a youth of 21 or thereabouts, who seemed in fierce excitement. He screamed to mamma, "Madam, I have come to liberate your people." Mamma replied, "I hope you will be kind to them. They are accustomed to consideration." This seemed to infuriate the little man, who shrieked, "That is a strange thing for a Southern woman to say to an officer of black troops."*

In another letter, Marion Porcher described the actions of the soldiers after their lieutenant told them, "Boys, take what you want":

Otranto Plantation. *Courtesy of the South Carolina Historical Society.*

All our stock, horses and mules were driven off, our cattle, sheep and hogs were killed; the barns and smoke-house were broken open, and all their contents scattered, and all our vehicles of every kind, tools and implements were broken in pieces and thrown into the creek or burned.

It was awful to hear the screams of cattle and hogs as they were chased and bayoneted, and the scatter and terror of the sheep was terrible to see. Even my pet calf…was killed; and dear old Aaron, our house cat, was cruelly run through with a bayonet, right before my eyes, as he tried to escape under the house. Such brutal scenes I never supposed I would ever have to witness.

Mamma said to Lieut J., who was looking with apparent pleasure at the scene of destruction, "If you deprive us of all means of subsistence we will starve." He turned and said, "You are now suffering for what you have done." Then, turning to the house servants who had gathered round us, he called Quash and said, "Uncle follow me." Quash said, "Yes, massa," at which the little man exclaimed, "For God's sake don't call <u>me</u> massa." He then summoned Fannie, Amy and Rachel, the house maids, and said "That woman (meaning mamma) is very wicked. I know she has hid things, you must show me where they are.

The rebel man has gone to the wars but he has left a damned rebel of a woman, and I want her head. Now show me everything." The maids protested that they knew of nothing concealed and that "miss" was not wicked...While this was transpiring upstairs Annie...and I were alone on the piazza facing a great crowd that surrounded the house and filled the whole yard and lawn. Indeed the scene of confusion was terrific...We saw an indiscriminate crowd of black and white with pointed bayonets come rushing towards the house evidently with the intention of entering.

Union general E.E. Potter soon showed up at the house to use it for temporary headquarters. When he found out that Mrs. Porcher was the sister of James Louis Petigru, a noted South Carolina unionist, he told her he would have "prevented the place from being molested." He soon learned, however, that she did not share her brother's political views but rather was a staunch Confederate.

After Philip J. Porcher's death in 1871, Otranto was purchased by a group of sportsmen that established a hunting preserve there.

PILLAGE AND DESTRUCTION OF THE COOPER RIVER PLANTATIONS

"What a Place to Plunder!"

In February 1865, the Confederate forces in Charleston were forced to evacuate the city, leaving it and the entire surrounding area defenseless. Charleston was quickly occupied by Federal troops, and regiments under the command of General E.E. Potter began raiding in the Cooper River region, an area filled with plantations.

In 1842, Dr. John B. Irving, a physician and South Carolina rice planter, wrote of the area along the Cooper River as it appeared before the war: "In proceeding up the river by the steamboat...there is very soon presented to the eye of the visitor, luxuriant fields, bearing on their ample bosoms, the rich staples of our country. On the left, as we ascend, several well settled farms, under high cultivation, are studded along the margin of the river."

Louisa Cheves Stoney, who edited and reprinted Dr. Irving's book *A Day on the Cooper River*, described how these rich farmlands and the homes of many wealthy, cultured planters were pillaged and vandalized by Potter's troops. This region "held much of the accumulated treasure of almost 200 years of peaceful prosperity," she wrote. "As Blucher said of London, 'What a place to plunder!,' and it was plundered for three months."

At Parnassus Plantation, the owner, Mrs. Tennent, waited fearfully with her daughters, knowing that Federal gunboats were steaming up the river. Soon soldiers in blue intruded on the family, demanding food and asking the whereabouts of valuables (which had been hidden by the Tennents). The soldiers went away but promised to come back the next night to dance with Mrs. Tennent's daughters, and she immediately left and took her family to a neighbor's plantation. In their absence, the house was looted, and when it was safe to return, Mrs. Tennent found her home completely bare. Hunger finally drove the family to move to Charleston.

John St. Clair White was only a boy of eleven when Potter's soldiers invaded his home at Gippy Plantation, occupied only by himself, his mother and one other lady. He remembered how the Federal troops arrived: "[T]he blue coats were literally pouring over the fence at the south and west fields." He recalled that they seemed more like a mob than an army. White went on to describe how the soldiers caught or killed all the poultry, loaded up all the stored foodstuffs and movable supplies to carry off and then pillaged the plantation house.

Dockon Plantation was the home of Colonel James Ferguson. Ferguson was elderly and blind, and late in the war he took his "family of females" to the nearby village of Pineville. Here, in February 1865, the Fergusons were driven out of their house, which was then burned by five soldiers, two of whom were officers. Many other houses in Pineville were also burned by Federal troops.

Louisa C. Stoney described how William James Ball, the owner of Limerick Plantation, prepared for Potter's raiders by hiding as many valuables as possible, mostly by putting them in the safekeeping of his slaves. When the Federal soldiers arrived, they plundered the plantation of almost all its livestock and supplies, leaving behind only one carriage. After the soldiers were gone, the ground was littered with papers, which turned out to be the magnificent illustrations ripped out of valuable books by John J. Audubon. The soldiers had used them as containers for their food.

Kensington Plantation, the home of Dr. John B. Irving, was thoroughly gutted. Whatever was not stolen was ruined or destroyed. In a letter of February 20, 1868, Dr. Irving described how some valuable family papers were lost, "scattered by Potter's command when they visited Kensington": "The soldiers broke into my study, saw the tin box, supposed it to contain money, knocked off the lock, and scattered all my papers of value on the lawn."

Irving and his son Aemilius later searched for some important property records they needed for legal purposes, but Aemilius reported in a letter to his father's lawyer that so far he had been unsuccessful in finding them and that they may have been "destroyed among many other papers at the time everything else in our house was pulled to pieces."

According to Charleston author Samuel Gaillard Stoney, many of the plantation houses were abandoned in the midst of the poverty and desolation that followed the war. Some of the landowners made a few attempts to plant rice and cotton again, but it eventually became too difficult to make a living growing either crop, especially after the arrival of the boll weevil. Stoney observed that even into the late 1920s, "the Low Country was a region of deserted fields growing up in forest, of ragged dying gardens and grim, cold, pathetic houses, solemnly awaiting their doom by fire or dilapidation."

DESTRUCTION OF THE LOWCOUNTRY PLANTATIONS

"The Demon of Civil War Was Let Loose"

Constance Fenimore Woolson, a Northern novelist who visited Charleston in 1875, wrote of the Ashley River area west of the city as it existed before the war: "The Ashley River, or 'up the Ashley,' was once the scene of great magnificence, the residences and the ways of living being modeled upon those of the English nobility."

Woolson went on to describe historic Drayton Hall, the splendid gardens at Magnolia and the ruins of Middleton Place ("once one of the most beautiful plantations in South Carolina"), and she also mentioned the "old Bull estate," better known as Ashley Hall Plantation.

William Izard Bull Jr. *Courtesy of the South Carolina Historical Society.*

When William Izard Bull (1838–1917) heard that South Carolina had seceded and that war was likely, he had just arrived in England, but he immediately returned to his native state and joined the Confederate army. Trained as a physician, he served as a surgeon in the First South Carolina Infantry Regiment and later with the Washington Artillery Battery.

He bore the same name as his father, William Izard Bull (1813–1894), who owned Ashley Hall near Charleston. During the American Revolution, the house there was looted by the British. Later, another war brought about its complete destruction, as Federal troops advanced into the area from the south. When William Izard Bull Sr. heard of their approach, he made the terrible decision to set fire to Ashley Hall himself rather than allow it to be pillaged and suffer a fiery fate at the hands of his enemies.

Ashley Hall was only one of many plantations along the Ashley River that were destroyed in the last year of the war. Almost all the others, including the beautiful estates of Magnolia and Middleton Place, were looted and burned by the U.S. forces. In an article published in 1866, Gabriel Manigault wrote of the latter:

> *Middleton Place, on the west bank of the Ashley River, the country house of this family for several generations, was perhaps the best known country residence in the state. It was remarkable for the extent and solidity though not the beauty of the mansion, the extensive terraces and shrubbery around it, and the treasures of literature, art and antiquity it contained, and for liberal and elegant hospitality from former times down to a late day, when the northern invaders sacked and fired it with more than Gothic barbarity. Among the property there, was a valuable service of plate carried to Russia by the late Henry Middleton, when U.S. Minister at St. Petersburgh, and brought back on his return to this country.*

Manigault added that an "old negro servant" hid these valuable pieces. When the soldiers arrived, they hanged him up by the neck several times, but he still refused to tell them where he had hidden anything and so "died with the secret undivulged." A similar incident occurred at Magnolia, where the owner's slave named Adam, a trusted and skilled manager and gardener, was strangled by soldiers seeking information on hidden treasures. While his sons watched his ordeal, Adam refused to give any information, and his torturers finally gave up and let him go.

Drayton Hall, one of only a few plantation houses on the Ashley River not burned by Federal forces. *Courtesy of the South Carolina Historical Society.*

Gabriel Manigault also noted that the beautiful house at Drayton Hall was almost burned—saved only because the Drayton family had a relative of high rank in the United States military:

> *The torch was about to be applied to it, when learning the name of the family that owned it, the enemy spared it for the sake of a certain commander in the U.S. Navy of the same name and family who having moved to the North was then busy, not in defending his own native State, but in the conquest and devastation of it.*

In an official report to the Episcopal Diocese of South Carolina dated 1868, Reverend Paul Trapier, the former rector of St. Andrew's Parish, wrote of the area:

> *Every residence but one, on the west bank of Ashley River, was burnt simultaneously with the evacuation, by the besieging forces from James Island. Many of these were historical homes in South Carolina; the abodes of refinement and hospitality for more than a century past…The demon of civil war was let loose in this Parish. But three residences exist in the whole space between the Ashley and Stono rivers. Fire and sword were not enough. Family vaults were rifled, and the coffins of the dead forced open in pursuit of plunder.*

The Bull family was prominent in the founding and early history of South Carolina and, for the most part, shared in its fortunes and misfortunes. Stephen Bull (circa 1733–1800) fought in the Revolutionary War, was a state legislator and owned large amounts of land, some in Prince William Parish, Beaufort District. The house he built at Sheldon Plantation was burned by British troops during the Revolution, rebuilt and burned again in 1865 by Sherman's troops. Nearly every plantation house in Prince William Parish was destroyed by Federal forces and their contents ruined or stolen.

An incident in the life of James Reeve Stuart, a relative of the Bull family, affords an example of looted items from the area showing up later in the North. After the war, Mr. Stuart became a well-known artist, and while visiting Chicago once on professional business, he heard that a "certain Union officer" who had served in South Carolina had some interesting portraits on display in his home. Mr. Stuart was given permission to see these artworks and was astonished to observe that they were paintings of his own ancestors—three portraits of Stephen Bull, William Bull Sr. and William Bull Jr.—all of whom he remembered well from seeing them many times during his childhood. They had obviously been taken from Sheldon Hall in Prince William Parish. When Mr. Stuart asked the owner who these men in the portraits were, the former Union officer replied that they were some of his ancestors. It was later reported that these paintings burned in the Great Chicago Fire that occurred not long after Mr. Stuart's visit.

MAYOR MACBETH'S PLANTATION IS BURNED

"A Heartless Act of Incendiarism"

Charles Macbeth (1805–1881) was a prominent lawyer of Charleston. During the war, he served as the mayor of Charleston, remaining in that office until 1865. When Charleston was evacuated in February 1865, Mayor Macbeth stayed behind and sent this message to the officer in command of the occupying Federal troops: "The military authorities of the Confederate States have evacuated the City. I have remained to enforce law and preserve order until you take such steps as you may think best."

Charles J. Macbeth in the uniform
of the Lafayette Artillery, 1861.
*Courtesy of the South Carolina
Historical Society.*

Upon his marriage to Henrietta Gourdin Ravenel in 1835, Macbeth came into possession of Wantoot Plantation in St. John's, Berkeley Parish (now part of Berkeley County). The house at Wantoot was built by Pierre de St. Julien in 1712. In 1781, during the American Revolution, British colonel Alexander Stewart made it his headquarters after the Battle of Eutaw Springs, where he had engaged the forces of General Nathanael Greene, the commander of the Southern Department of the Continental army.

In late February 1865, while Macbeth was in Charleston, Federal forces under the command of Union generals E.E. Potter and Alfred S. Hartwell were involved in expeditions into surrounding areas, including nearby Berkeley County. During this time, Mayor Macbeth's house was burned. In his memoir about St. John's, Berkeley Parish, Professor Frederick A. Porcher wrote:

Mr. Macbeth was guilty of several heinous crimes. He was mayor of Charleston; he had sons in the army of the Confederate States, who had distinguished themselves; and the stern justice of General Potter condemned Wantoot house to the flames. It was a heartless act of incendiarism, executed in cold blooded malice, when not a Confederate soldier was to be found within a hundred miles.

Charles Macbeth had four sons who served in the Confederate army. Charles J. Macbeth served in the Lafayette Artillery and the Twenty-seventh South Carolina Infantry Regiment. James Ravenel Macbeth, a captain in the First South Carolina Artillery Regiment, was imprisoned at Johnson's Island (Ohio) for more than a year and, after returning to active service, lost an arm in battle. Richard Yeadon Macbeth served in the engineer corps, and his younger brother, James Gaillard Macbeth, joined the Rebel Troop in 1864 at sixteen years of age.

The ruins of the house at Wantoot could be seen for many decades after the war. The entire plantation was inundated in the early 1940s, along with many other historic properties, when two vast man-made lakes were created as part of the Santee Cooper Project.

The Burning of Orangeburg

"One Heap of Ashes"

On February 12, 1865, about six hundred Confederate soldiers attempted to defend the Midland town of Orangeburg from the onslaught of Sherman's army, but overwhelmed by a vastly larger force, they were compelled to withdraw toward Columbia, and the Federals crossed the Edisto River and took possession of the place. Major Oscar L. Jackson of the Sixty-third Ohio Infantry Regiment recorded in his diary that the Federal soldiers who first entered Orangeburg found a store in flames and claimed that it had been deliberately set on fire by its owner, a Jewish merchant. "A fine breeze was blowing," wrote Jackson, "and by the time we got into the town there was a big hole in the center of it and our boys rather assisted [the fire] than stopped its advance."

A woman watching from a building facing the public square, however, had a different view of what happened. From a window, she had seen a "blue-clad" soldier climb up to the roof of Mr. Ezekiel's store and set it on fire with a torch (possibly one of the "bummers" who were almost always in advance of the main army). Her nephew, a young boy named Thomas O.S. Dibble, also watching from a nearby window, saw the town's volunteer fire company (a group of old men and boys) trying to put out the flames and then observed Union soldiers cutting the leather fire hose through which they were pumping water.

Reporter David P. Conyngham was an eyewitness to the destruction:

> *Orangeburg…had been a pretty place before the war, and had a population close to two thousand…When I reached the city, it was in flames…by the following morning one heap of ashes. The tasteful churches, with their tall steeples, and about fifty private houses, alone escaped. It was a sad sight the next morning to witness the smoking ruins of the town, the tall, black chimneys looking down upon it like funeral mutes, and to see old women and children, hopeless, helpless, almost frenzied, wandering amidst the desolation.*
>
> *The Orphan Asylum is somewhat in the rear of the town, and then contained over two hundred children. It was presided over by a New York lady…a very sensible lady, who talked freely about the present troubles. Her sympathies were with the south. She felt very keenly for her helpless charge, now that the railroads are torn up, and the country devastated.*

The orphans had been sent to Orangeburg from Charleston to keep them safe from the Federal bombardment of the latter place.

Mrs. Augustus Jennings recorded her mother's memories of the invasion of the Orangeburg area, describing how the lady recalled the Union soldiers pouring into their plantation a few miles from the town, Oak Grove, acting "like maniacs, yelling and hurrahing, breaking open doors…Some of the negroes were screaming with fright and some were exultant. One faithful house servant was whipped until she disclosed the hiding place of silver and other family treasures." When Mrs. Jennings's mother tried to protest the ransacking of her house, an officer from Ohio advised her to be quiet, "for if the soldiers were enraged, he could not answer for her life." Mrs. Jennings went on to state that "everything of value was stolen or burned, including the clothing," and that an old, retired family horse that refused to pull the soldiers' stolen buggy full of loot "was beaten unmercifully" by them. She added that this kind of "vandal warfare" left her family's plantation "a field of want and despair."

Sherman's forces arrived in Orangeburg on a Sunday, and the last of them left on the following Tuesday, by which time they had also burned down the courthouse. In the Episcopal *Diocesan Records* published in May 1865, the minister at the church in Orangeburg, commenting on the poverty in his parish resulting from the invasion, reported that "most of the few who were well off among his parishioners are now poor; that widows and orphans, who had saved a little from the wreck of their property in the low country, are stripped of that little, and that defenseless females were living on the scraps left by those who had taken from them their supplies for domestic use."

Chapter 2
The Burning of Columbia, February 1865

MARY C. WEST AND HER FAMILY ARE
WARNED ABOUT COLUMBIA

"Don't Go There of All Places"

In her later years, Mrs. Mary Cheves West of Charleston wrote out a brief affidavit that she entitled "Statement in Reference to Burning of Columbia." In it she recalled her family's encounter with General Sherman and two of his officers in Savannah, Georgia:

> *Soon after the evacuation of Savannah by the Confed[erate] army, in 1864, and its possession by the Federal army, two of Gen. Sherman's staff officers, Capt. Dayton of N.J. and Col. Poe of Ohio, occupied, at my mother's request, a room in our house, at the corner of Bull & Jones Sts.*
>
> *One evening Gen. Sherman after making these two gentlemen a visit, sent one of them up to know if it would be agreeable to us, to receive him. My mother answered that she would be pleased to do so. Accordingly the general came up to our parlor bringing in his hand a history of Georgia, from which he proceeded to read to us…After some further conversation he went on to say, that when he crossed the river into S. Carolina, he would leave <u>no</u> home standing, letters from "the <u>good</u>, the church going people of the North," telling him not to leave a house standing in that state.*

The right wing under General Howard crossing the Saluda River.

Some weeks after, as well as I remember, Col. Poe, who was a polite & friendly foe, as he was about to leave, came to say good-by to us. He found my aunt Mrs. John Cheves, with her daughter, were to go…into the Confederacy, and he asked her into what part of the country she was going. When she answered "Columbia" where her friends were, he responded earnestly, "Don't go <u>there</u> of all places. <u>We</u> are going there."

I was present upon both of these occasions, and think I have reported the conversation correctly.

THE ALLEN HOUSE IS BURNED

"Nothing but Blackened Chimneys"

Mrs. Fannie E. Allen looked back on her family's terrible experiences in Columbia in 1865 and wrote out an account of "those facts which were stamped indelibly on my mind at the time":

Several thousand women and children, a handful of men, eighty-four squares of beautiful dwellings. Such was Columbia on February 14, 1865. On February 15, General Sherman and an army of sixty thousand men occupied the banks of the Congaree, on the Lexington side, and in two days the city presented the appearance of having passed through a rain of fire.

The shelling of the city commenced early Thursday morning. The shells fell thick and fast, in every direction, the arsenal and the State House furnishing conspicuous marks. One fell directly at my mother's feet, but, fortunately, the fuse had been extinguished, and the missile did not explode. The sudden attack and the fear of what was to follow rendered us numb with fear, and we scarcely had power to take ourselves to a place of safety.

Fortunately, my father, just home from the army, although nearly dead with consumption, was with us, and we felt more secure than thousands of others less fortunate.

After an almost sleepless night, we were startled about daybreak by a loud explosion. Hastily dressing and getting out, we learned that the South Carolina warehouse had been blown up, and the wildest rumors were afloat as to its cause.

The "swish-swish" of the pontoons being laid for the army to cross told us that Sherman intended entering the city at once. In less than an hour afterward the work of pillage and destruction commenced. Drunken soldiers, the worst corps in the army, had been sent over, accompanied by drunken negroes, staggering around, insulting women and children, and taunting them with their helplessness. Darkness, that which we worst feared, fell, and with it began the crowning deed of all. A blaze was seen a little way off; the fire bell began to ring. Soon another blaze was seen, then another, until the whole town was a mass of flames. Soldiers, now crazy with drink, began to look for something more valuable than food or clothing. Houses were entered, and jewelry, gold and silver, plate—anything of value—was taken. This did not happen in every case. At some house an officer would stop, and that house was generally safe, as the officer would throw a guard around it. Such cases, however, were rare.

As the fire drew nearer our house on Assembly Street, we began to move the household effects out. A Yankee soldier, half drunk, came by and, seeing a trunk, wanted to open it. My brother, about fifteen years of age, attempted to stop him, but was silenced with an oath, and the trunk was smashed in and rummaged through.

With our house burned, we would have fared badly, but our neighbor, Mrs. T.B. Clarkson, who came over for protection, with her baby, had the servants to erect a kind of shelter with a few boards, and under this we stopped for the rest of the night. Sleep was impossible and, half dead with fright, we huddled under these boards, waiting for daybreak.

The scene that greeted our eyes the next day was heart-breaking. On every side, where there had once been handsome dwellings, were nothing

Columbia as it was first seen by the approaching Federal army.

but blackened chimneys, and in the streets were women and children, weeping over their homes and not knowing where the food for that day was to come from.

The Taylor house, afterwards known as the Haskell place, for some reason was not destroyed, and, along with several others, we took refuge there. The few men in the city took charge of all the food and established a sort of commissary, where supplies were issued several times a day for several days, until outside supplies were received.

MISS JORDAN IS WARNED OF COLUMBIA'S FATE

"And He Told Me the City Would Be Burned Tonight"

Catherine Jordan, a native of Cork, Ireland, was for many years a beloved servant in the family of Reverend William H. Barnwell of Beaufort, South Carolina, and after she left the family's employ, she kept in touch through letters. In 1865, she was living in Columbia, South Carolina. On March 15, 1865, the Irish lady wrote this letter to a daughter of Reverend Barnwell, relating, among other things, that on the late afternoon of February 17, a Yankee soldier warned her that Columbia was to be burned that night:

General Sherman's entry into Columbia.

My dear Miss Catherine,

I have received your kind and welcome note…My dear friend, all I have possessed on earth, and all my little mementoes of forty years gathering was burned on Friday night by General Sherman's Army in less than two hours…[T]he shelling was very rapid. While I was preparing my trunks…one [shell] burst on the side of the little house. Still I felt not afraid, but I was trying to get one trunk spared for me, and two Yankee soldiers came in and asked [for] bread and meat as usual. I had none prepared, and immediately they cursed me, being in liquor, and another came and asked for needle and thread, which I gave with a kind heart, and seeing nobody with me, he told me there will be a great deal of trouble tonight. I said, how soldier? And he told me the city will be burned tonight, and he said, I wish you could get somebody to stay with you. With that, he bid me goodnight, and in going out he called to me to look at the fire commenced already; that was about six o'clock. So I put on my hat to go to Mrs. Trumbo to get a guard for me. Every step with fear and trembling with the yells of the drunken soldiers…

I could not get help…[my house] was plundered first and then set on fire and in ashes before I got back again and not one thing was saved, but what was on my back…Poor Columbia is desolated. It is a night I will ever remember. I was on the green all night and somebody gave me a blanket to cover me. It was so cold, and the cruel Yankee came and took it from me and put it on his horse and the same to the Doctor Goodwin's lady.

Miss Jordan later lived in Charleston, South Carolina, and died there on February 3, 1874, at the age of sixty-three. One of Sherman's generals, William B. Hazen, stated in his memoirs: "I have never doubted that Columbia was deliberately set on fire in more than a hundred places."

HORRORS IN COLUMBIA

"We Are in the Hands of Our Bitter Enemies"

In a memoir, Mrs. Sarah Henry Bryce of Columbia described the arrival of Sherman's forces and the beginning of the end for the capital city of Columbia in February 1865: "When they reached the Broad River they commenced shelling the city, and continued doing so during the day without demanding its surrender...The enemy crossed the river on pontoon bridges on the memorable morning of the 17th."

The mayor and three aldermen went out with a white flag to surrender the city and were assured by one of Sherman's officers, and later by the general himself, that Columbia would be safe. Mrs. Bryce went on: "At that time there was no fire visible in any part of the town. We relied on his [Sherman's] word, but soon found we were leaning on a broken reed."

Reverend Robert Wilson, an Episcopal clergyman, reported in a letter to a relative that he was in the streets of the city just after Sherman's troops entered the city and that the soldiers began their pillaging that morning. "Many persons were robbed publicly early in the day," he wrote, adding, "And how shall I attempt to describe the horrors of that fearful night? It is useless to make the effort. Hell was empty, and all its devils were in this devoted city...A perfect reign of terror existed."

Trying to keep her family and possessions safe, Mrs. Bryce managed to secure guards for her house:

> *About dusk I saw three sky-rockets, red, white, and blue, go up. I asked one of the guards what that meant. He shook his head, and said, "Don't ask me; you will know soon enough."*
>
> *In a very short time I saw fires springing up all around the city. The citizens brought out the fire-engines and hose; but they were quickly rendered useless by the Federal soldiers, who cut the hose with axes and stuck their bayonets in them. Our people soon realized that it was all premeditated, and it was useless to resist. They destroyed the engines, pierced and cut the hose, destroyed the water-works and then the gas-works. We were in the hands of our bitter enemies, without engines or water and in black darkness, except for the lurid light of our burning houses.*

The two Federal soldiers guarding the Bryce family were soon overwhelmed by a crowd of others that had come to rob the house, and Mrs. Bryce was forced to leave with her children and servants and go into the "bitter cold" and streets "filled with blue coats" who were delighting in "a perfect carnival of robbery and pillage."

Reverend Robert Wilson reported in the same letter mentioned earlier: "Numbers of houses were fired in the very presence of sick women and children, one I know, where a lady had an infant two hours old."

South Carolina author William Gilmore Simms described some of the more horrific aspects of the night, noting first the rapes of black women by the soldiers and then their mistreatment of white women and even the dead:

> *The poor negroes were terribly victimized by their assailants, many of them…being left in a condition little short of death. Regiments, in successive <u>relays</u>, subjected scores of these poor women to the torture of their embraces…*
>
> *A lady, undergoing the pains of labor, had to be borne out on a mattress into the open air, to escape the fire. It was in vain that her situation was described as the soldiers applied the torch within and without the house, after they had penetrated every chamber and robbed them of all that was either valuable or portable. They beheld the situation of the sufferer, and laughed to scorn the prayer for her safety.*
>
> *Another lady…was but recently confined. Her condition was very helpless. Her life hung upon a hair. The men were apprised of all the facts in the case. They burst into the chamber—took the rings from the lady's fingers—plucked the watch from beneath her pillow, and so overwhelmed her with terror, that she sunk under the treatment—surviving their departure but a day or two…*
>
> *In several cases, newly made graves were opened, the coffins taken out, broken open, in search of buried treasure, and the corpses left exposed.*

A Mr. McCarter of Columbia reported similar atrocities, recording in his journal how "frightened negro women sought protection & places of refuge against the lustful soldiery" and adding that the "bodies of several females were found stripped naked & with only such marks of violence upon them as would indicate the most detestable of crimes." In his observations, McCarter likened the Federal troops to crusaders.

"'This glorious Union' constantly on their lips," he wrote, "they wanted to reestablish the Union even if by doing so they annihilated the present population."

A Columbia physician, Dr. Daniel H. Trezevant, recorded several horrible instances of rape in notes he kept about the burning of the city. One took place at a house where Federal soldiers seized Mrs. Thomas B. Clarkson Jr. "and forced her to the floor for the purpose of sensual enjoyment." She resisted "and held up her young infant as a plea for their sparing her." The soldiers relented but took her maid instead and, in Mrs. Clarkson's presence, raped her on the floor. Mrs. Clarkson and her infant daughter were then turned out into the cold. Dr. Trezevant also recorded how a female slave belonging to Reverend Peter Shand was brutally raped and then murdered by seven soldiers who "held her head under the water until her life was extinct."

In his history of Sherman's march, Burke Davis related that one of Sherman's staff officers, Colonel Dayton, reported that he had shot a man who was attempting to rape a white woman in the streets of Columbia.

August Conrad, a German cotton buyer who had the misfortune of being in Columbia in February 1865, took refuge in the house of some friends, but soldiers set fire to it despite the presence of a guard. As the family fled the house, Mr. Conrad caught one soldier setting fire to a bed in which an elderly woman lay. He recalled in his memoir:

> It was a matter of great difficulty to save the old grandmother, who escaped death by fire by a hair's breadth, and was carried out by two negroes who were kind enough to lend a helping hand. I caught one of the noble heroes by the throat at the moment when he was about to set fire to the bed on which the old lady lay, because I had run thither at her shriek of horror and stopped, just at the right time, fearful murder. In the struggle, which in view of this incredible crime I did not fear…I found out, to my horror, that the beast was a German who could not even speak English.

Conrad also noted the mistreatment of other defenseless females, recalling that the soldiers "did not restrain themselves till the opening of the jewel cases, but lacerated the ears and tore off the clothing from the bodies of the trembling women. I have myself seen a lady with the lobes of her ears torn asunder."

New York newspaperman David P. Conyngham, traveling with Sherman's army as a correspondent, described the terrible ordeal of the people of Columbia and was himself almost killed in an attempt to save a citizen from being murdered:

> *I trust I shall never witness such a scene again—drunken soldiers, rushing from house to house, emptying them of their valuables, and then firing them; negroes carrying off piles of booty…officers and men reveling on the wines and liquors, until the burning houses buried them in their drunken orgies.*
>
> *I was fired at for trying to save an unfortunate man from being murdered.*
>
> *The frequent shots on every side told that some victim had fallen. Shrieks, groans, and cries of distress resounded from every side. Men, women, and children, some half naked, as they rushed from their beds, were running frantically about, seeking their friends, or trying to escape from the fated town. A troop of cavalry, I think the 29th Missouri, were left to patrol the streets; but I did not once see them interfering with the groups that rushed about to fire and pillage the houses.*

William Gilmore Simms also recounted an instance of murder during Columbia's occupation. The mayor of the city, while walking through the streets of Columbia with General Sherman, heard a gunshot, and both men went to find its source. They found a group of Federal soldiers standing over the dying body of a young black man, and Sherman asked them, "What does this mean, boys?" A soldier replied that the "damned black rascal" had been impudent to them, so they shot him. The general ordered his men to bury the body at once. Sherman was asked, "Is that the way, General, you treat such a case?" The general replied, "We have no time now for courts martial and things of that sort!"

Edward L. Wells, a cavalryman, was one of the Confederate soldiers forced to retreat from Columbia. On the night of February 17, 1865, he and fellow soldiers were encamped in the countryside about seven or eight miles from the city. Of this Wells later wrote:

> *A chilly wintry night was succeeded by a gloomy leaden gray dawn. As the cavalrymen aroused themselves a strange sight met their half-blinded*

The burning of Columbia.

eyes. Great clouds of heavy black smoke were drifting through the camp, and their horses in alarm were straining uneasily at their halters. At first it was supposed, that the woods in the neighborhood were on fire, but investigation soon proved that this was not the cause. Then the solution of the terrible phenomenon broke upon the men in a horrible revelation; it was the smoke from burnt Columbia. Heartrending and baffling description was the scene then witnessed. The poor fellows realized that thousands of women and children, among them their nearest and dearest, were crouching, roofless and foodless, in the pitiless winter air, or had met a worse fate. Groans were extorted from strong men, and tears wet the cheeks of grim veterans.

In her *Recollections of the War*, Mrs. Mary S. Whilden wrote of what she believed was an attempted murder:

At the time of Sherman's raid on Columbia, I had an infant who, from exposure, contracted a severe cold and was threatened with a serious illness. I took the child to an army doctor whose headquarters were in the Preston mansion…and asked for medicine. I stood on the front balcony, which was draped with the United States flags. The doctor cursed me as a rebel woman, and said, "Let the d----- rebel die." I told him I would make a record of what a United States officer had done...Still a further piece of villainy awaited me. On the campus of the Presbyterian Theological Seminary there was quartered another surgeon, with a number of soldiers, so with hope of better results I went to him. He received me very courteously, and with my request for medicine he handed me a phial, directing that I should administer to the child a teaspoonful. I did not examine what the bottle contained till I returned to my room, when to my horror I discovered it was laudanum. Can you imagine a more diabolical act?

Laudanum was an opiate, which may have proved fatal to an infant.

PROFESSOR LECONTE AND SHERMAN

"The Streets Were Filled with Ten Thousand Yelling Soldiers"

Joseph LeConte (1823–1901), a native of Georgia, was skilled in a number of scientific disciplines. Educated at Harvard University and elsewhere, he was the professor of chemistry and geology at South Carolina College in Columbia from 1857 until 1869, when he moved to California. In 1892, concerned about the preservation of the Sierra Nevada mountain range, LeConte became one of the founders of the Sierra Club.

Of the momentous events that began in the South in 1860, Professor LeConte wrote in his autobiography:

This secession movement was first called an insurrection, and later a rebellion; and the war that followed is commonly spoken of...as "the War of the Rebellion." Nothing can be more absurd. The Confederate States composed a thoroughly organized government, as much so as the United States. During the whole war the machinery of government was practically perfect. It was a war between the States, or better still, a war between two nations. For each side it was really a foreign war...let it be distinctly understood, that there never was a war in which were more thoroughly enlisted the hearts of the whole people—men, women, and children—than were those of the South in this. To us it was literally a life and death struggle for national existence.

In 1864, when the armies of General Sherman were sweeping through Georgia, Professor LeConte traveled there to rescue his daughter Sallie, who was trapped behind enemy lines. A journal he kept of his exciting and harrowing adventures eluding Sherman's army, which included several narrow escapes, was published as 'Ware Sherman. In February 1865, the professor managed to make his way back to Columbia, where the rest of his family had endured the horrors of the sacking and burning of the city in their house on the college campus:

I entered the city at the extreme Northern end, and went down the whole length of the main street, a mile and a half. Not a house was standing and I met not a living soul! The beautiful city, the pride of the State, sat desolate and in ashes. The fire had swept five or six blocks wide right through its heart, leaving only the eastern and western outskirts. At last I saw the brick wall surrounding the campus of the College, and a few minutes later was knocking at the door of my own ivy-covered home. Deep silence for a moment, then the quick pattering of little feet along the hall, then my wife and children hanging around my neck with mingled laughter and tears.

Then followed a recital of experiences on both sides. Theirs had been far more dreadful than mine, but as I did not personally witness them I shall not attempt to describe the terrors of the bombardment of the sixteenth and seventeenth, the still greater terrors of the entrance and occupation of the enemy, or the inconceivable horrors of the night of the seventeenth. But a few facts I learned from my wife and daughters and later confirmed by thousands of eye-witnesses, I will briefly state.

Our forces evacuated the city early on the morning of the seventeenth, the Yankees entering and taking formal possession about nine o'clock. General Sherman personally promised the Mayor, Dr. Goodwyn, complete protection and perfect security of personal property, and during the day everything was quiet. A number of officers, however, among them a colonel quartered in my brother's house, hinted about certain rockets that would signal the destruction of the city. About seven in the evening, after ten hours of peaceable possession, when there were no Confederate soldiers within fifteen miles, these signal rockets went up from various parts of the city and instantly fires burst out everywhere. In an hour Columbia was a roaring, surging sea of flames. The streets were filled with ten thousand yelling soldiers, running from house to house with flaming torches, and even stealing their trinkets from the frightened women who rushed into the streets from their burning homes. Every house in the city, except those within the campus walls, was pillaged, and most of them first pillaged and then burned.

The LeConte family remained in South Carolina for several more years, until Professor LeConte could no longer bear what came after the war, which he described as "worse than the war itself." First it was the military rule of the state by Federal troops, and then it was the carpetbagger regime. "The iniquity of the carpet-bag government," he wrote, "was simply inexpressible." In 1868, LeConte applied for employment at the new University of California in Berkeley. He was elected to a professorship (in geology, natural history and botany) and moved there in September 1869.

Professor LeConte's daughter Emma also kept a diary during the war. In it she wrote of how the soldiers exulted in the destruction of the city and that though at first they tried to make excuses for the fire, one of them frankly admitted that "Sherman had ordered them to burn it, that they expected to burn it, and that they *did* burn the hole of secession." Emma LeConte's passionate, compelling account of her experiences during the burning of Columbia was published in 1957 as *When the World Ended.*

LOUISA S. McCORD AND HER FAMILY

"That Was an Awful Night"

Louisa S. McCord (1810–1879), a noted author and intellectual of her time, has been recognized as one of the most significant thinkers of antebellum America. The mother of three children, she owned and managed Lang Syne Plantation in St. Matthew's Parish near Columbia and wrote poetry, reviews, a blank verse drama entitled *Caius Gracchus* and numerous essays on political economy and other subjects. She also translated a book written by Frédéric Bastiat, a French political economist, which was published in 1848 as *Sophisms of the Protective Policy.*

Though devastated by the death of her only son, Langdon Cheves McCord, who died as a result of wounds received at the Battle of Second Manassas, she devoted herself to feeding and clothing soldiers and nursing the wounded in the military hospital in Columbia. She was the president of the Soldiers' Relief Association and the Ladies' Clothing Association of that city.

Mrs. McCord owned a house in Columbia that General O.O. Howard, Sherman's second in command, used as his headquarters when the city was occupied by U.S. forces on February 17, 1865. Just before Howard arrived, a crowd of Federal soldiers began ransacking and pillaging the place. One of them seized Mrs. McCord by the throat, throttled her and tore a watch from her dress. When General Howard arrived, the soldiers were still at work, and Mrs. McCord wrote that the general saw these men in the very act of looting.

A little while later, Howard caught some of his own men attempting to set fire to the McCord residence. He ordered them to stop, but when he saw that Mrs. McCord was nearby and had overheard him, he approached her and laid the blame on the burning cotton "flying about." On another occasion, when a ball of burning cotton was found inside an entryway of the house, General Howard commented again that it was remarkable how the cotton was blowing about, and Mrs. McCord answered him, "Yes, General, very remarkable, through closed doors."

Earlier that same day, she had received an ominous note urging her and her family to leave Columbia:

> *One of my maids brought me a paper, left, she told me, by a Yankee soldier; it was an ill-spelled but kindly warning of the horrors to come, written upon a torn sheet of my dead son's note book, which, with private papers of every kind now strewed my yard…The writer, a lieutenant of the army of invasion, said he had relatives and friends at the South, and that he felt for us; that his heart bled to think of what was threatened. "Ladies," he wrote, "I pity you; leave this town—go anywhere to be safer than here." This was written in the morning; the fires were in the evening and night.*

In a letter penned on March 21, 1865, Mrs. McCord's daughter, Louisa (later Mrs. Augustine T. Smythe), described the family's ordeal as Columbia was occupied and soldiers entered their yard:

General Oliver Otis Howard.

We bolted upstairs ready for them & well it was we did, for in a short time the yard was crowded with these vile creatures on foot & on horseback, kicking open doors, picking locks & altogether tearing up the place about as effectually as it could well be done. They stole everything—literally everything that could be carried—actually stuffing lard into their pockets. Everything not to be carried was smashed...Knowing that they would kick the door down in no time, Mamma unbolted it & then they just over ran the house she just following them to keep them from the stairs... Just in the midst of all the fuss down stairs, while Mamma was having a nice time, one of the men having pushed her up against the wall and dragged her watch off, while another flourished a handful of stolen knives in her face, and all the rest behaved themselves in somewhat the same way, stealing & smashing & were at last beginning to look up stairs, some one rang the bell & in walked Gen. Howard & his staff come to look for quarters.

In the evening, young Louisa went out to the upper porch of the house to see what was happening outside:

The McCord house, which still stands as an historic property in Columbia. *Courtesy of the South Carolina Historical Society.*

We seemed almost surrounded by the flames and with the wind blowing so furiously we thought it impossible that any house should escape... That was an awful night... it was a horrid feeling to be so at the mercy of these men when you could see how they rejoiced at all their work. The whole night long there was a most horrid confusion. Yells & curses worse than all their horrid laughter & jokes, & then by way of adding to it they were throwing shells & hand grenades about the whole night. Crowds of women and children gathered in the park & the Yankees actually stood on the hill above & threw hand grenades among them.

In his notes about the events of that same night, Dr. Daniel H. Trezevant similarly reported of the soldiers: "They threw fireballs among the women & girls who had sought shelter in the park."

After the war, a committee of citizens was appointed to collect testimony concerning the burning of Columbia by Federal troops. More than sixty affidavits from eyewitnesses, including Mrs. McCord, were assembled. They were presented, along with the committee's report, to the mayor of Columbia in November 1868, but these records inexplicably disappeared from the municipal archives during the Republican (i.e., carpetbagger) administration of the city. When a search was made for the original report and affidavits in 1878, they were nowhere to be found.

THE MIDDLETON FAMILY

"The Better Men and Officers Were Ashamed of Themselves"

Harriott Middleton (1828–1905) was the fourth daughter of Henry Augustus Middleton (1793–1887), a wealthy South Carolina rice planter of the Georgetown District. She and other female members of her family were living in Columbia when the city was besieged by General Sherman's forces. About ten days after the burning of the city, she penned a letter to her cousin, Susan M. Middleton (1830–1880), recounting her recent experiences. After reporting that Susan's black servant Henry had been severely beaten and robbed by Federal soldiers, Harriott went on:

I do not think I can pretend to tell you anything of the days after you left and after the Yankees entered. Wednesday and Thursday were visionary days. There was a wild hurrying to and fro, pale agitated faces, intolerable anxiety, painful rumors, shelling of the town, cannonading advancing and then receding, at times musketry firing was distinctly heard. We thought that nothing could be worse. Alas, we little knew what fate had in store for us.

Harriott's aunt managed to secure a guard, Corporal Morris, for their house. When a nearby house caught fire, the Middleton ladies moved their beds and other belongings outside into a garden, but the corporal soon advised them to go back inside:

He had been weeping constantly all the evening and very kind. At length he said, "I will tell you the truth. I have saved your house so far, but I cannot stay much longer and your house will be in ashes before morning. Not one house is to be left in Columbia. Do you not see there are no guards in the streets, the city is given up to the soldiery? Go with your things into the garden if the house catches. I will stay with you and guard you as long as I can, but I must soon leave you to your fate. Do not go into the streets."

I will tell you when I see you how we seized upon him and declared he should never leave us. The kind-hearted man was appalled by the fate he believed was in store for us and it was no wonder we were alarmed by his terror for us. We all went into the dining room, which was crowded with bedding, trunks, etc…and we waited together the ending of a night of horror…

The soldiers rushed about with pots of turpentine in one hand and pine sticks in the other. Others had bundles of straw and lightwood torches. They say that in the burnt district the scenes were fearful with the drunken soldiery and helpless women and children…The men we saw told us that it was the most appalling night in their experience of war. The better men and officers were ashamed of themselves before morning. They said, "This is a perfect Hell!" "What a fiendish piece of work" and such like expressions.

Corporal Morris, watching a neighbor's house burn, turned to Harriott and said, "If I saw any rebels burning down my home as all of you are seeing us burning down yours, I would hate them all my lifetime, and never afterwards give quarter to them in battle. I would kill all of them."

The house that the Middletons occupied was not burned, but the next morning, the ladies went out to witness incredible destruction all around them. In the same letter, Harriott also wrote about a pregnant friend, Anna Raven Vanderhorst Lewis (1830–1865), who "died of the Yankees":

She was in a very agitated state all the time they were here. It brought on a premature confinement and she and her baby left this world of trouble within forty-eight hours. If her excitement could have been lessened, if she could only have slept, her life would have been saved, but nothing could bring her rest. The whole time the Yankees were here she was in fear and trembling...Poor Raven! She showed so much unselfishness and kind thoughtfulness of others during and before her illness. She leaves six little children to mourn a most devoted and affectionate Mother. It is another in the long list of Yankee enormities.

In March 1865, Harriott's elderly father joined his family in Columbia, having walked much of the way from his Georgetown District plantation, Weehaw, which had been raided by soldiers of a New York regiment. Harriott wrote to her cousin Susan about this, expressing her great distress over the burning of the family home and the loss of a beautiful garden that had been cultivated and loved by her brother, Francis (Frank) K. Middleton (killed in the war in May 1864). In letters written in March 1865, Harriott reported:

Then Weehaw is gone, lying in ashes. Papa walked up here though he got many a lift on the road. I mourn over Frank's garden as I would over a dear friend, and the Yankees cut down the oak trees everywhere. Susan I know now what it is to hate! I believe the destruction of Frank's garden has taught it to me...

I don't think I told you in my last [letter] the polite way in which Papa was turned out of his house. Capt. Pierce of the 157th New York Volunteers thus addressed him "You damn old rebel you, get out of your house this minute. I mean to burn it down and set you afloat in the world." Then he took his bonds, money and everything else he found and burnt the house.

REVEREND ANTHONY TOOMER PORTER

"It Seemed as Though the Gates of Hell Had Opened Upon Us"

Anthony Toomer Porter (1828–1902), a native of Georgetown, South Carolina, was an Episcopal priest who served as a chaplain in the Confederate army for most of the war. In 1864, he returned to Charleston to minister at the Church of the Holy Communion, but in February of the following year, he and his wife and family were forced to evacuate Charleston and go to Columbia. In his autobiography *Led On! Step by Step*, Reverend Porter described their experiences there. On the morning that the Federal army entered the city, the clergyman happened to see General Sherman and engaged him in a conversation. Among other things, the general told him to "go and tell the ladies they were as safe as if he were a hundred miles away":

> *I went home and told the ladies at Dr. Reynold's house, to which several families in their alarm had fled for refuge. It was about half-past eight at night, when I told the ladies what General Sherman had said, and they only replied, "Do you believe him? Go on to the roof of the house and see for yourself."*
>
> *A Captain of the Federal army had billeted himself on us, and was welcomed by us, as we thought he could protect the house. This officer went with me to the roof of the house, and we there saw that the whole of Columbia was surrounded with flames. I pointed this out to the Captain, and said I believed they were going to burn Columbia.*
>
> *"No," he said, "those are camp-fires."*
>
> *I told him that I had been four years in camp, and thought I knew what a camp-fire was. Then I pointed out several residences on fire... The environs of the town were ablaze. Then a fire broke out in Main Street, near Hunt's Hotel, caused by an overturned lamp in a saloon, which ignited the liquor, and as the flames spread, two or three small hand-engines were brought out which I saw Federal soldiers work on. Suddenly three fire-balloons went up, and in ten minutes eight fires broke out simultaneously across the northern street of the city, about equal distance from each other, and stretched almost entirely across the town.*
>
> *At once the men who had been on the engines a moment before turned in and broke them to pieces. I saw this from the roof of the house.*

"See that?" I said to the Captain.

He gave one long look, then darted down the skylight, and we never saw him again.

A gale of wind was blowing from the north that night, and that soon caused the fire to burn freely, so that in a short time the city was wrapped in a lurid sheet of flames. Coming down from the house, I told the family that their fears had just become realized.

"Columbia is being burned by the enemy."

Reverend Porter went out into streets for a while to observe what was happening in the city:

Going into the street I there beheld a scene which, while memory lasts, I can never forget. Streams of pale women, leading their terrified children, with here and there an infant in arms, went by, they knew not whither, amid the fierce flames…The streets were filled with soldiers mounted and on foot, in every stage of drunkenness…Shouts of derision and blasphemy filled the air. Cries of "There are the aristocrats!" "Look at the chivalry!" were yelled into the ears of these defenseless women. Men seemed to have lost their manhood, and the mere beast was in the ascendant…Amid all this confusion there were occasional explosions of ammunition and shells, as the fire reached their places of storage. The bursting of barrels of liquor, the falling of brick walls, the howling of the wind, for it was blowing a gale, and the swish of the flames leaping wildly from house to house mad a terrific uproar. I, myself, saw men with balls of cotton dipped in turpentine enter house after house. Some would take bottles of turpentine, throw the liquid round about, and then set it afire. It seemed as though the gates of Hell had opened upon us.

Later, after taking his family to a place near the houses that the Federal officers were using as their headquarters, Reverend Porter went out into the streets again. For a second time, he saw General Sherman, who blamed the burning of the city on South Carolina's governor:

"Why did not your Governor destroy all this liquor before he left? There was a very great quantity of whiskey in the town when we arrived."

"The drunken men have done much," I replied, "but I have seen sober men fire house after house."

Reverend Anthony Toomer Porter.

After the general passed on, Reverend Porter was accosted by three soldiers. One of them struck the clergyman on his head and ripped off a shawl that he was wearing. Porter described what happened next:

The three had not gone far, when another Federal soldier who had just come across the river, and had not been in the riot, came up and said, "Stranger, I saw that man strike you, and steal your shawl; it is an outrage." Dropping his gun from his shoulder he continued: "I am ashamed this night to own that I belong to this army; I enlisted to fight and preserve this Union; I did not come to free negroes, or burn down houses, or insult women, or strike unarmed men. Stranger, I have a mother and two sisters," and raising his right arm towards Heaven as he leaned upon his gun, he said, "Oh, my God, what would I do if my mothers and sisters were in such a plight as these poor women are in here to-night. Stranger, if I were a Southern man in sight of this burned city, I would never lay down my arms, while I had an arm to raise."

The officer retrieved Reverend Porter's shawl for him, and a little while later, the clergyman was aided by another Federal officer, Lieutenant John A. McQueen, who had protected the Porter family in his absence.

The Ravenel Family

"We Saw Our Conquerors"

Harriott H. Ravenel was the wife of Dr. St. Julien Ravenel, and in her personal narrative about the burning of Columbia, she described the awful decision she faced as Sherman's army approached the city:

> *Dr. Ravenel was then the chemist in charge of the very large laboratory in the Fair Grounds buildings, where were prepared almost all the drugs, medicines, styptics, etc., used by the army, and also a quantity of alcohol and whiskey—for medical purposes only. The first thing that showed us how near the danger was was an order from Richmond, "Prepare to remove all chemical and medical stores to some convenient point in North Carolina. Chemist in charge to go with them and establish a laboratory as soon as possible, wherever he may find suitable." We at once considered as to what was to be done. Probably every other woman in Columbia was considering the same question. Shall we go, or shall we stay?*
>
> *To go meant horrible discomfort. To stay meant—we did not know quite what! For ourselves I promptly decided to stay. It would have been almost impossible to move such a family as ours single-handed—and clearly Dr. Ravenel could not go with us. We had no shelter elsewhere provided, and we, like most other families, had already laid in stores of provisions and fuel which it would have been impossible to move, and very bad to leave behind. Altogether, to us to stay seemed best, though many of our friends decided otherwise…*
>
> *The laboratory train was to go in the morning, and we had to remain. For the next three days, it was nothing but going—vehicles of every kind and trains loaded with every conceivable thing. We busied ourselves with bringing into the house, and storing in the upper rooms, whatever we could…*

At last...we heard the sound of guns across the river, and knew that Sherman was approaching, shelling as he came...The shells did not at first reach us, but they fell thickly enough around the State House and college buildings, then used as a hospital. I was on the front porch early in the morning, listening to the guns, when I saw a buggy, driven by a servant, stop at the front door. A young lady, who looked very ill, was lying back in it, with a baby in her arms; and the servant called out to ask if I would take them in, as their house was under fire, and they had been obliged to leave it. Of course I brought them in, and found the baby was only one week old and the mother much exhausted. We did what we could—put them in my own bed, fed, kept them quiet, and the young mother soon revived.

The following morning, a servant came to Mrs. Ravenel's house to announce that "the Yankees were going down Main Street":

We went to the street in front and looked westward, and saw crossing it an endless blue column, with glittering arms, and flags flying in all the pomp of war. Our spirits sank, for we saw our conquerors...Our first trouble came about an hour after the entrance, when two horsemen rode into the yard, and came into the house, saying they had come to look for arms. Of course they found none. I had a pistol, but it was safely hidden. But they ransacked the house and helped themselves to all the small things they fancied—whatever they could put into their pockets or holsters...At last they rode off, assuring us that they would call again.

Later, in the evening, successive waves of plundering soldiers entered the Ravenel house and frequently attempted to set fire to it:

The glare of the burning town was awful, and I expected at every moment to be consumed. The servants behaved admirably, and repeatedly extinguished fires which had been set in the kitchen and outbuilding. We had to watch the sheds, for a man would snatch up a book, kindle its leaves at his torch, and throw it out of a window, and we should have been in flames many times if we had not got out at once on the piazza roof and extinguished the blaze...Our preservation came, I think, from their desire for plunder. To plunder first, and then burn, was their plan. So they did not set fire until they were leaving (they came in gangs), then they would throw a torch or a handful of blazing paper into a closet, or behind a curtain, and go, before the next set came in, and that saved us; but it was dreadfully fatiguing work.

As Sherman's army departed Columbia a few days later, Mrs. Ravenel watched, knowing for certain that these men were responsible for the terrible destruction they left behind:

When the immense column of men, cannon and baggage wagons filed past us, on its way to North Carolina, it seemed like a world in arms. Last of all came the mounted guard, looking into every house and yard to see if any straggler might be concealed there. But stragglers there were none, or few, for the admirable discipline of General Sherman's army cannot be too highly estimated. They greatly mistake who attribute the horrors of that night to accident or insubordination. The skillful commander held them in the hollow of his hand, and said to them, "So far shalt thou go, and no farther."

SOPHIA SOSNOWSKI OBSERVES THE BURNING OF COLUMBIA

"We Could Hear the Cries and Lamentations"

Sophia Wentz Sosnowski (1809–1899), a native of Germany, was the daughter of Christian Wentz, court physician to the Grand Duke of Baden. She came to New York with her husband, Joseph S. Sosnowski, a captain in the Polish army, shortly after their marriage in 1833. After her husband's death in 1845, she turned to teaching to support her children, and she eventually moved her family to South Carolina. Just before the war, she took over the South Carolina Female Collegiate Institute at Barhamville, about two miles north of Columbia, where she distinguished herself as a teacher of languages, literature and vocal music. Also known as the Barhamville Academy, this well-known school attracted young ladies from prominent families of South Carolina and other states.

During the war, Madame Sosnowski devoted herself to the care of sick and wounded soldiers, and her students set aside time each week to make clothing for the Confederate troops. She recorded her memories about

The South Carolina Female Collegiate Institute at Barhamville. This image of the school appeared in an advertisement in the *Daily Southern Guardian*, a Columbia newspaper, in 1861. *Courtesy of the South Carolina Historical Society.*

Sherman's army in Barhamville and Columbia in an extensive memoir entitled "The Burning of Columbia: A Thrilling, Faithful & Graphic Description of a Monstrous Crime." Learning of the enemy's intentions to take Columbia, Madame Sosnowski sent her pupils into North Carolina and the upstate for their safety, but she remained at Barhamville with some others. Soon, from the roof of the school building, they could plainly see the city in flames, especially after nightfall:

> *Columbia was then enveloped in one sheet of flame; we could hear the cries and lamentations of the people, even at this great distance. It was a terrible night! Soon the building of Capt. A., whose wife and sister had taken refuge with us, was set on fire by the soldiers… The scenes enacted at that dwelling in connection with the negro servants are not fit for female pen to dwell upon…The negroes informing the soldiers of some valuable wines stored away, thus was given the signal for general bacchanalia. When the intoxicated servants disclosed to the reveling soldiery the hiding place of the*

family silverware and other valuables, the tumult reached its
height...At last the negroes themselves became thoroughly disgusted,
and although enriched by the booty the soldiers could not carry off...
they vowed vengeance for the base treatment their women had been
subjected to.

Dr. Marks, the founder of the Barhamville Academy, managed to procure guards to protect the school, but their presence was not enough to keep out numbers of soldiers who intruded on Madame Sosnowski during the night and on the following day:

Drunken and infuriated soldiers, some with saber in hand, endeavored
to open the side doors. Another hour brought a party of soldiers who
were inclined to harangue us on political questions. One among
them...made a regular stump speech, in which he endeavored to
demonstrate that this country was destined only for the white man,
and that the Indian, as well as the negro, had to be, or in the course
of events would be, exterminated; furthermore, he expressed his own
wish to have the entire negro race on an immense platform and power
sufficient to blow them all to atoms. This latter remark was received
with repeated cheers by his companions-in-arms.

When her guards left, Madame Sosnowski walked to Columbia to see if she could obtain the same kind of protection for her school. She went to the headquarters of the occupying army and managed to secure an interview with General Sherman, whom she addressed boldly and candidly:

I stated to him...my indignation at the course the army had pursued towards
a conquered, unresisting and surrendered city. I told him further that...in a
civilized country battles would be fought, but private property and females
would be protected, but instead of this a warfare was waged which would
make it a disgrace to our present history.

The angered general responded by blaming the secessionists for their own sufferings and concluded by saying, "You have suffered much already, but if I have to come back again..." He left his threat unfinished and told her that she had no further need for a guard as his army would be leaving soon.

After the war, Madame Sosnowski moved to Athens, Georgia, where she became the principal of the Lucy Cobb Institute. She later operated her own school there, known as the Home School, until the year of her death.

THE RUIN OF A POET

"Beggary, Starvation, Death, Bitter Grief"

Henry Timrod (1828–1867), a poet, essayist and editor, began his brief and tragic life in Charleston. At the age of eighteen, he went to study law at the University of Georgia but withdrew before completing his studies. Returning to South Carolina, this brilliant, passionate young man soon decided that he was not cut out to be a lawyer. He tried to obtain employment as a college professor but, finding no position available, became a private tutor. While making a living in this way, Timrod began to write poetry that was published in the *Southern Literary Messenger* and other periodicals. During holiday breaks, he spent most of his time in Charleston, where he became part of a select circle of literary men that included the famous writer William Gilmore Simms. A book of Timrod's poems was published in 1860, and although favorably received, it was soon overshadowed by momentous political tensions and the beginning of the war.

Though poor health kept Timrod out of active military duty and soon led to his discharge, he did enlist. He was detailed to clerical work and later served a brief stint as a war correspondent for a Charleston newspaper in 1862.

In 1864, Timrod was profoundly disappointed when a project to publish an illustrated edition of his poems in England fell through. That same year, he moved to Columbia, South Carolina, to become editor of the *South Carolinian*, a daily newspaper. Shortly after his arrival there, he married Kate Goodwin, a young Englishwoman who inspired his beautiful poem "Katie." On Christmas Eve 1864, a son was born to the couple, but Timrod's brief period of happiness came to an end when Columbia was reduced to ashes by General Sherman's army in February 1865.

Impoverished and ill, Timrod struggled to support his wife and child, as well as six dependent relatives. In October 1865, he was devastated by the death of his infant son, and his health began to deteriorate rapidly. The family survived on the charity of neighbors and friends and by selling off their few remaining possessions.

Timrod wrote to a friend in March 1866: "You ask me to tell you my story for the last year. I can embody it all in a few words: *beggary, starvation, death, bitter grief, utter want of hope*! You know, I suppose that the Sherman raid destroyed my business. Both my sister and myself are completely impoverished. We have lived for a long period, and are still living, on the proceeds of the gradual sale of furniture and plate."

In October 1867, at less than forty years of age, Timrod died from tubercular hemorrhages. Before his death, the poet suffered for weeks. Though his case was very serious, he hoped for recovery, but eventually his physician told him that there was no chance of it. When the poet's sister tried to comfort him by saying, "Darling, you will soon be at rest," Timrod answered, "Yes, but love is sweeter than rest."

On the morning of his death, his wife attempted to give him some water, but he was unable to swallow it. "Never mind," he told her, "I shall soon drink of the river of eternal life." Those were his last words.

During the war, Henry Timrod wrote a series of patriotic verses for which he became known as the "Poet Laureate of the Confederacy." One of his last poems was an ode to commemorate the graves of the Confederate dead at Magnolia Cemetery in Charleston.

The Burning of the Catholic Convent in Columbia

"What Do You Think of God Now? Is Not Sherman Greater?"

At the age of seventeen, Selina Bollin was a pupil at the school of the Ladies' Ursuline Convent in Columbia. She wrote an account of her experiences during the Federal sack and occupation of the city in which she described what happened to the Ursuline nuns and the young girls in their care, recalling how "rowdy soldiers" attempted to break into the convent.

Toward nightfall, the Mother Superior, Baptista Lynch, went up to the cupola of one of the buildings, from which she had a good view of

Father J.J. O'Connell.

the city. Earlier, she had sought and received a written assurance from General Sherman that the convent would be protected, but she soon ran down the stairs with the news that the convent was "doomed." The nuns bundled their pupils in habit cloth to protect them against the cold and had them line up in an orderly procession to leave the building. Some of the girls were as young as seven years old—the youngest was only five.

Father Jeremiah J. O'Connell, a priest who led them out, recalled:

> *It was never dreamt that a civilized country would deem it expedient in the hour of midnight to fling out into the flames of a burning city, abandoned to the pillage of a dissolute soldiery, inflamed with the worst passions of the human heart, a body of venerable and worthy ladies, with their band of little children, and all of the first and most respectable families, both Sisters and their pupils. I led that mournful procession from the desecrated Convent, through the lurid flames, to the graveyard of the church.*

Just before the schoolgirls and nuns left with Father O'Connell, a crowd of soldiers broke down the chapel door and entered the sanctuary. One of

Views of the ruins of Columbia.

the pupils, Mrs. Sara A. Richardson, who was a girl of eighteen at the time, recalled what happened as the girls were praying with one of the nuns:

> *While we were on our knees, we were brought standing by the most unearthly battering in of the chapel door behind us, and reached by a stairway from the Main street side. It was like the crash of doom. Drunken soldiers piled over each other, rushing for the sacred gold vessels of the altar, not knowing they were safe in the keeping of one blessed of God…Curses and threats filled the Convent when they found the gold chalice had escaped their polluted hands.*

Fortunately, the altar vessels had been taken away earlier and hidden by another priest. Although the chapel was saved due to the intervention of some soldiers, the convent was destroyed; it was plundered before it was burned by the soldiers. One of the nuns recorded in a letter that the pillage "commenced at about midnight." The soldiers even broke into the convent dormitories: "Hatchets and crowbars came into play, and doors soon gave way. The handsome dresses of the pupils were thrown all over the courts; books, music, etc., were tossed in every direction, and the trunks broken and emptied."

As the procession of females led by the priest moved through the burning streets, the heat was so intense that Selina Bollin's cloth gaiters (leggings) were scorched as she walked. They found a place of refuge in a graveyard, where the girls could hear the frightened "howls and shrieks" of the inmates in the State Hospital, an asylum for the insane.

Sara A. Richardson described the burning of the convent: "Soldiers were seen with torches to fire it from the roof. Some of the ruder soldiers asked the good nuns, as they watched their home being destroyed, 'What do you think of God now? Is not Sherman greater? Do you think now you are sanctified? We are as sanctified as you.'"

The next morning, as some officers were riding through the streets, the Mother Superior recognized General Sherman and confronted him with the plight of the nuns and children in her care who were now homeless. Reminding the general of his broken promises, she managed to get him to agree to give the nuns one of the houses "left standing." They chose the Preston mansion, which was being used as the headquarters of Union general John A. Logan, and took refuge there.

Chapter 3

After Columbia: Into the Midlands and the Upstate, February–March 1865

THE TRAPIER FAMILY'S ORDEAL IN CAMDEN

"I Could Fill Pages"

Reverend Paul Trapier (1806–1872) was born at an estate called Belvedere near Charleston. He was of French Huguenot extraction, and his grandfather of the same name (Paul Trapier, 1749–1778) was a Georgetown planter and a delegate to the Continental Congress. Reverend Trapier graduated from Harvard in 1825, studied for the ministry in New York and was ordained as a priest in the Episcopal Church in 1830.

In 1833, he married Sarah Dehon Russell, and for most of their married life, they lived at her mother's fine home on Meeting Street, today known as the Nathaniel Russell House. All of their twelve children were born here. Reverend Trapier served as the rector of St. Michael's Church for six years in the 1840s, and about two and half years before the war began, he was elected to a professorship at the newly established Episcopal Theological Seminary in Camden, South Carolina. Here the Trapiers purchased a large home just outside town called Kamchatka (or Kamschatka), formerly owned by James Chesnut and his wife, Mary Boykin Chesnut, the famous diarist. The theological seminary was shut down in June 1862 after all the students had enlisted in the Confederate army.

Kamchatka, as it appeared toward the middle of the twentieth century. *Courtesy of the South Carolina Historical Society.*

After leaving much of Columbia in ashes in February 1865, Sherman's forces moved northward, and at Liberty Hill, South Carolina, General John A. Logan divided his Fifteenth Corps into two columns and sent a detachment from one to raid Camden to the south.

The reporter David Conyngham, who was with this detachment, described Camden as "a beautiful town" and stated that the first Federals to arrive there on February 23 was a small group of "foragers" who "skirmished with some cavalry, driving them into the town, and, following them, soon took possession of it."

The "cavalry" was a small group of militia composed of old men and boys. Conyngham reported that the next morning, larger detachments were sent into Camden that "destroyed all government property, public stores, the depot, and some public buildings." The men also destroyed "about fifty thousand rations of corn meal, and four thousand bales of cotton" in Camden.

An article published in the Camden newspaper described Sherman's soldiers as having "run through the gamut, from impertinence to outrage, from pilfering to wholesale spoliation. Many families have been stripped of everything they had in the world. In one neighborhood, where they unearthed buried liquor, they were especially riotous and fired houses with wanton cruelty."

The Trapiers were one of these families robbed of nearly everything of value that they owned, including the gold seal of Reverend Trapier's grandfather and a brooch containing the hair of Mrs. Trapier's late father, Reverend Theodore Dehon, the Bishop of South Carolina. Their son, Theodore, a soldier at home recovering from a severe illness, was taken prisoner and forced to march with Sherman's army into North Carolina, where he nearly died.

Within months of these events, Mrs. Trapier wrote an account of their ordeal, describing in detail the systematic pillage of their house by the soldiers, the threats and insults to which her family was subjected and her desperate anxiety for her family and servants. Some of the soldiers went into a bedroom, where her youngest daughter, Edith, was sick in bed. The child, who was only about twelve years old, became "violently agitated" as the men began to search under the covers of her bed. Her father, who had followed them into her room, exclaimed, "Don't you see how the child is troubled?" When Edith burst into tears, the soldiers relented, but not without searching the rest of the room, even probing under the child's bed, before leaving. One of the men pulled opened a trunk and found a Confederate cap in it. "Whose is this?" he asked, and when Reverend Trapier told him that it belonged to his son, the soldier replied, "Your son's in the artillery. A bullet for him."

Later in the day, some of the soldiers became intoxicated from some liquor they had found elsewhere in town, and their behavior grew more menacing. That night, when the raiders finally left the house, Mrs. Trapier experienced some relief, but no one in the household felt safe. "The frightened servant girls ran to us for protection and slept all night in our nursery," she wrote.

Never shall I forget that night! We separated into two parties, one keeping watch in the parlour, the other in the room of the sick child. The little children, huddled together, wrapt in blankets on the floor, forgot their sorrow in uneasy slumbers. It was raining incessantly, and as our fires burned out and we did not dare to go for more wood, those of us who were in the parlor suffered from cold…

Towards morning at my husband's persuasion, while he watched I threw myself on the bed and slept from sheer exhaustion. I awoke at daylight, and hastened to the window. Not a vestige of the enemy was to be seen. But flames rising in different parts of the horizon, shewed how they were employed. About breakfast time kind enquiries from the neighbours with sad, sad accounts of robbery, insult and drunkenness poured in…

I could fill pages with accounts of the misery these raiders left in their track. Their treatment of the slaves…was atrocious. A gentleman in our neighborhood assured us that not a female slave on his plantation (with a single exception) was allowed to retain that which should have been dearer to her than her life. This exception, a brave married woman, stood at the door of her house with a log of wood in her hand, and said she would dash out the brains of any man who came near her.

In June 1865, Mary Boykin Chesnut visited Kamchatka, her old home, and participated in a prayer meeting there led by Reverend Trapier. She wrote, "I do not think I ever did as much weeping or [was] as bitter in the same space of time…He prayed that we might have strength to stand up and bear our bitter disappointment, to look on our ruined homes and desolated country, and be strong." They also prayed for Confederate president Jefferson Davis, who had been put "in a dungeon and in chains."

For the next five years, Reverend Trapier struggled to support his large family, finally accepting a position as rector of a parish in Maryland in 1870. His health began to fail the following year, and in 1872, he died. His wife, Sarah, passed away in 1889. Both are buried in the cemetery of St. Michael's Episcopal Church in downtown Charleston.

SHERMAN'S TROOPS IN WINNSBORO

"My Soldiers May Do as They Please!"

After the destruction of Columbia, a wing of Sherman's army moved across the Saluda and Broad Rivers, destroyed the Greenville and Columbia Railroad for about thirty miles and then moved on into Fairfield County. William W. Lord (1819–1907), a Northern-born clergyman and poet whose writings had been praised by William Wordsworth, was the rector of the Episcopal church in the town of Winnsboro at the time. In a memoir, his son recalled how the townspeople sent Reverend Lord as an emissary to General Sherman. Reverend Lord met with some of Sherman's officers, who conveyed the clergyman's plea for mercy to their general:

> *This* [plea] *was to the effect that as Winnsboro contained no cotton held in storage and sheltered only helpless women and children, the army on its march be not be permitted to burn and pillage it.*
>
> [Sherman's] *reply came quick and terse: "Burn and pillage be damned! My soldiers may do as they please!"*
>
> *My father protested indignantly against what he called an eleventh-century answer to a nineteenth-century appeal; but he was promptly warned back to silence by the remark of a staff officer, that gentlemen of his cloth had been sent North in irons for saying less...A passport through the Union lines was handed to him, and a promise was made that the headquarters of General Sherman and his staff would certainly be fixed within the residential part of the village, which would avail to save the rectory.*
>
> [The] *advance-guard of unofficered and undisciplined stragglers... rode along our little street without making any depredations or paying any attention to the closed shutters and doors of the frightened villagers; for the pioneers seemed to know that their conquering general—"Uncle Billy," as they fondly called him—was to make his headquarters on that street... Downtown, however, the torch was soon applied by the main body of the army, which had entered the village by another road, and the business portion of Winnsboro was at once wrapped in flames. Like truants out of school, these overgrown "Boys in Blue" played snowball along the fire-lit streets with precious flour; made bonfires of hams and sides of bacon...set boxes and barrels of crackers afloat on streams of vinegar and molasses that were sent flowing down the gutters from headless barrels; and fed their horses from hats filled with sugar, throwing what remained into the flames or the mud. In this wanton horseplay enough foodstuff was destroyed to have nourished the community abundantly for at least a year.*
>
> *While high carnival was held thus amid the burning stores downtown, the residential sections of the village were not neglected. All homes outside the sacred limits of the headquarters precinct were stripped of food and treasure...*

Winnsboro, South Carolina.

That the conflagration was at last controlled was due to the intervention of Brigadier-General Slocum, of New York. Claiming that an extension of the fire line might endanger the headquarters residence, he organized a bucket brigade of bluecoats and saw to it that "Uncle Billy's" house and the public buildings escaped the flames.

General Ario Pardee of the 147th Pennsylvania Regiment reported: "The town was filled with foragers from different corps of the army. These men, in the most unlicensed manner, had plundered the public and nearly all the private residences, and to the same body may be charged the firing of the town." In an official letter reporting on his division's activities in Winnsboro, Union major general John W. Geary noted that "acts of pillage and wrong to defenseless inhabitants were committed by foragers...we had daily evidence."

Between twenty and thirty buildings in Winnsboro were burned, including St. John's Episcopal Church. A report submitted to the Episcopal Diocese of South Carolina by its "Committee on the Destruction of

Churches" contained the following statements concerning the Winnsboro church building:

> *This church was wantonly burned by Sherman's troops on their march through Winnsboro. The public square was destroyed, but the Church was not touched by that fire. It was on the outskirts of the town in a large lot, and was deliberately set fire by the soldiers, after the central square was consumed. The organ, furniture, books, and all the Church property perished.*

While the church burned, soldiers exhumed a new grave and split open the coffin with an axe, exposing the corpse. The body was that of Alfred Manigault, a member of the Charleston Light Dragoons, who had died of spinal meningitis in Winnsboro the day before the city's capture. Alfred's brother, Louis Manigault, preserved a letter from a friend, Edward Horlbeck, who informed him that some of Sherman's soldiers had taken his brother's body out of his grave and put a potato in his mouth, while others carried the organ out of the church to play music and dance around it as the building burned. Horlbeck also expressed his regret that he had not known of Alfred's presence in Winnsboro before Sherman's arrival. "I did not hear anything about him," he wrote, "until after the Great Incendiary Sherman passed and permitted such acts to be perpetrated by his followers *the scum of the nation.*"

A year later, in February 1866, the Manigault family removed Alfred's body from St. John's cemetery and reburied him at St. Philip's churchyard in Charleston.

A few days after some of Sherman's forces left Winnsboro, on February 27, 1865, a black woman who lived in a cabin on the Catawba River (part of which forms the eastern boundary of modern Fairfield County) was raped and tortured by two soldiers of the Thirty-eighth Ohio Volunteers, Private Thomas Killgore and Private Daniel Kunkle. The two men were court-martialed and found guilty. Killgore was sentenced to ten years hard labor, and Kunkle received the same penalty for four years.

REVEREND JOHN BACHMAN'S HARROWING EXPERIENCES IN CHERAW

"A System of Torture Was Practiced"

Dr. John Bachman (1790–1874) was a naturalist of international reputation and a beloved Lutheran clergyman. He was a native of the state of New York and was called to the pulpit of St. John's Lutheran Church in Charleston in 1815. A friend of the renowned naturalist John James Audubon, Bachman collaborated with him to produce *The Viviparous Quadrupeds of North America* (published in three volumes, 1845–49), providing much of the scientific data that informed Audubon's beautiful paintings. Bachman authored numerous books on science and religion, served as the professor of Natural History at the College of Charleston from 1848 to 1853 and helped to found Newberry College, as well as the Lutheran Theological Southern Seminary in Columbia. In December 1860, he was one of the ministers chosen to offer the opening prayer at South Carolina's Secession Convention. He regretted the dissolution of the Union but thought that it was better for the two sections of the country to separate, like Abraham and Lot, when they could no longer live together in peace.

When General Sherman's army invaded Cheraw, South Carolina, Dr. Bachman was in the area, staying at a place called Cash's Depot, and about six months later, he wrote a lengthy letter about all that he saw and experienced there. The following is an excerpt from his letter dated September 14, 1865:

> *I witnessed the barbarities inflicted on the aged, the widow, and young and delicate females. Officers, high in command, were engaged tearing from the ladies their watches, their ear and wedding rings, the daguerreotypes of those they loved and cherished. A lady of delicacy and refinement, a personal friend, was compelled to strip before them, as they might find concealed watches and other valuables under her dress. A system of torture was practiced toward the weak, unarmed, and defenseless, which, as far as I know and believe, was universal throughout the whole course of that invading army. Before they arrived at a plantation, they inquired the names of the most faithful and trusted servants; they were immediately seized, pistols were presented at their heads; with the most*

Reverend John Bachman.
*Courtesy of the South Carolina
Historical Society.*

*terrific curses, they were threatened to be shot if they did not assist them
in finding buried treasures. If this did not succeed, they were tied up and
cruelly beaten. Several poor creatures died under the infliction. The last
resort was that of hanging...They were strung up until life was nearly
extinct, when they were let down, suffered to rest awhile, then threatened
and hung up again. It is not surprising that some should have been left
hanging so long that they were taken down dead. But it was not alone
the poor blacks (to whom they professed to come as liberators) that were
thus subjected to torture and death. Gentlemen of high character...gray-
headed, unconnected with the military, were dragged from their fields or
their beds, and subjected to this process of threats, beating, and hanging.
Along the whole track of Sherman's army, traces remain of the cruelty
and inhumanity practiced on the aged and defenseless. Some of those who
were hung up died under the rope, while their cruel murderers have not
only been left unreproached and unhung, but have been hailed as heroes
and patriots.*

Dr. Bachman went on to describe how the slaves, male and female, were treated by the soldiers:

> *On Sunday, the negroes were dressed in their best suits. They were kicked, and knocked down and robbed of all their clothing, and they came to us in their shirt-sleeves, having lost their hats, clothes, and shoes. Most of our own clothes had been hid in the woods. The negroes who had assisted in removing them were beaten and threatened with death, and compelled to show them where they were concealed. They cut open the trunks, threw my manuscripts and devotional books into a mud-hole, stole the ladies' jewelry, hair ornaments, etc., tore many garments into tatters, or gave the rest to the negro women to bribe them into criminal intercourse. These women afterward returned to us those articles that, after the mutilations, were scarcely worth preserving. The plantation, of one hundred and sixty negroes, was some distance from the house, and to this place successive parties of fifty [soldiers] at a time resorted for three long days and nights, the husbands and fathers being fired at and compelled to fly into the woods.*

Dr. Bachman, who was about seventy-five years of age, was robbed of his watch by Federal soldiers. They repeatedly questioned him about the location of other valuables, and when he did not answer to their satisfaction, one of them beat him so severely that one of his arms was paralyzed for the rest of his life. A few weeks later, Dr. Bachman happened to encounter this same soldier, now a captive held by outraged Confederate militiamen who were eager for revenge:

> *They were excited to the highest pitch of rage, and thirsted for revenge. They believed that among the prisoners that had just arrived on the railroad-car, on their way to Sumter, were the very men who committed such horrible outrages in the neighborhood. Many of their houses had been laid in ashes. They had been robbed of every means of support. Their horses had been seized; their cattle and hogs bayoneted; their mothers and sisters had been insulted, and robbed of their watches, ear and wedding rings. Some of their parents had been murdered in cold blood. The aged pastor, to whose voice they had so often listened, had been kicked and knocked down*

by repeated blows, and his hoary head had been dragged about in the sand. They entreated me to examine the prisoners and see whether I could identify the men that had inflicted such barbarities on me. I told them I would do so, provided they would remain where they were and not follow me. The prisoners saw me at a distance, held down their guilty heads, and trembled like aspen leaves. All cruel men are cowards. One of my arms was still in a sling. With the other I raised some of their hats. They all begged for mercy. I said to them, "The other day you were tigers—you are sheep now." But a hideous object soon arrested my attention. There sat my brutal enemy—the vulgar, swaggering lieutenant, who had ridden up to the steps of the house, insulted the ladies, and beaten me most unmercifully. I approached him slowly, and, in a whisper asked him: "Do you know me, sir?—the old man whose pockets you first searched, to see whether he might not have a penknife to defend himself, and then kicked and knocked down with your fist and heavy scabbard?" He presented the picture of an arrant coward, and in a trembling voice implored me to have mercy: "Don't let me be shot; have pity! Old man, beg for me! I won't do it again! For God's sake, save me! O God, help me!" "Did you not tell my daughter there was no God? Why call on him now?" "Oh, I have changed my mind; I believe in a God now." I turned and saw the impatient, flushed, and indignant crowd approaching. "What are they going to do with me?" said he. "Do you hear that sound—click, click?" "Yes," said he, "they are cocking their pistols." "True," said I; "and if I raise a finger you will have a dozen bullets through your brain." "Then I will go to hell; don't let them kill me. O Lord, have mercy!" "Speak low," said I, "and don't open your lips." The men advanced. Already one had pulled me by the coat. "Show us the men." I gave no clue by which the guilty could be identified. I walked slowly through the car, sprang into the waiting carriage, and drove off.

By not identifying this man as his assailant, Dr. Bachman probably spared his life.

Assault and robbery were not the only crimes committed against Dr. Bachman by Sherman's soldiers; he also saw a lifetime of research and collecting destroyed by them:

I had been collecting a library on natural history during a long life. The most valuable of these books had been presented by various societies in England, France, Germany, Russia, etc., who had honored me with membership, and they or the authors presented me with these works, which had never been for sale, and could not be purchased. My herbarium, the labor of myself and the ladies of my house for many years, was also among these books. I had left them as a legacy to the library of Newberry College, and concluded to send them at once. They were detained in Columbia, and there the torch was applied, and all were burned. The stealing and burning of books appear to be one of the programmes on which the army acted. I had assisted in laying the foundation and dedicating the Lutheran Church at Columbia, and there, near its walls, had recently been laid the remains of one who was dearer to me than life itself. To set that brick church on fire from below was impossible. The building stood by itself on a square a little built up. One of Sherman's burners was sent up to the roof. He was seen applying the torch to the cupola. The church was burned to the ground, and the grave of my loved one desecrated. The story circulated, that the citizens had set their own city on fire, is utterly untrue, and reflects dishonor on those who vilely perpetrated it. General Sherman had his army under control. The burning was by his orders, and ceased when he gave the command.

In a paper about Bachman written in 1903, Reverend Michael R. Minnich noted, "Dr. Bachman's whole library and all his collections on Natural History, the accumulation of the labors of a long and industrious life, were burnt by the Federal Army during the Civil War... The loss to the scientific and historical world by this piece of vandalism cannot be estimated."

Always a man of delicate health, Dr. Bachman returned after the war to his pastorate at St. John's Lutheran Church in Charleston, where he ministered as best he could for about another six years. In January 1870, he occupied the pulpit for the last time to preach his fifty-fifth anniversary sermon.

MARGARET H. ADGER'S PLANTATION IS PLUNDERED

"The Yard Was Filled with Lawless Soldiery"

Margaret H. Adger (1820–1915) was the widow of Charleston businessman William Adger (1816–1853). Two of her sons served in the Confederate army. In May 1864, her son Andrew wrote to her hoping that his regiment would be sent north "to see the war carried home to the Yankees, as it has been too long to us. It is time for them, now, to have a turn in the horrors of war. It makes one's blood boil to hear of the devastation created by them."

To escape the bombardment of Charleston, Mrs. Adger took her daughters and servants to a farm near Hartsville, in Darlington County, South Carolina. Here, in February 1865, the family was subjected to some of the "horrors of war" in the form of several successive raids by Sherman's soldiers. Mrs. Adger wrote about them in a memoir:

> *When the Yankees were in our house, I asked one if he had been there when Columbia was burning. "Columbia, did you say Columbia? Once there was such a city, but you will never see Columbia again!" Such a look of triumph in his eyes as he thus spoke to me…Our house and premises were filled with invaders rushing in every direction and stealing everything they could find…*
>
> *The next day, before breakfast time, they came in numbers, alarming and bewildering us…The invaders rushed in and out of every part of the house and premises, emptying every drawer, trunk, closet, etc., and injuring or destroying what they could not carry off—even from the wash kitchen our wet clothing from the tubs and stealing all they could from our servants. They gathered up every Bible and hymn book they could find, took them out of doors and tried to burn them…I went as soon as that squad departed and pulled out of the flaming pile my son Andrew's handsomely bound hymn book, almost destroyed…*
>
> *The next morning…as usual, [I called] in the colored children for family worship, which was scarcely finished when several "Federals" rode up, alighted, hitched their horses and tramped into the house. Then came another day, even worse than yesterday's acts.*

Sherman's bummers "foraging."

Though terrified, Mrs. Adger was convinced that her family was under divine protection, remembering biblical verses concerning God's special concern for widows and the fatherless. She related how, after she read some scripture aloud in front of the soldiers setting fire to the farm's outbuildings, they decided to spare her house. After this group left, however, another one arrived:

> *That whole band had gone. But now we heard hoofs approaching, and a fresh company of Yankees reined up…The yard was filled with lawless soldiery…my attention was diverted by one demanding the key of an outhouse. In this we had tried to hide our soldier boys' trunks and some other precious things…I saw them force the trunks open. At the sight of the uniforms once worn by my son-in-law in the Citadel Academy they set up an Indian yell. Then one garment after another they took, piling them on their arms. "They are my son's clothes," I said, "which they do not need, but which we expect to give to our negro boys." "What do you care for negroes," one observed. "Are you not fighting for the negro?" [I asked]. "No, we are fighting for the flag. Your boys are lying on some battle field," and carrying his armful off he sang, "Who Will Care for Mother Now?"*

One soldier who had not participated in the pillage apologized to Mrs. Adger for the conduct of the soldiers in his army but explained that "there was no restraint" put on their activities.

After all the soldiers left, she remembered that "a tablespoonful of chipped beef was all that we had for that day. The next day a kind old neighbor brought us a bag of meal. Thus we were provided for."

The scorched hymnbook Mrs. Adger rescued from the flames is still in the possession of the family.

BESSIE PRINGLE'S DIARY, 1865

"They Delight in Making Terrible Threats of Vengeance"

Elizabeth W. Allston (1845–1921), later Elizabeth Pringle, was the daughter of Robert F.W. Allston (1801–1864), a wealthy rice planter and agriculturalist of Georgetown District, as well as governor of South Carolina from 1856 to 1858. Bessie, as she was called, was born on Pawleys Island and was only sixteen years old when the war began.

In 1863, fearing for his family's safety, Mr. Allston moved them to Croly Hill, a farm in Darlington County, South Carolina, while he remained at his plantation, Chicora Wood. At Croly Hill, the Allston family lived in reduced circumstances, gardening to put food on the table and making their own clothes.

In April 1864, Robert F.W. Allston succumbed to illness. The following year, the fatherless family, consisting of Bessie, her mother and her sister, Adele, were terrified when Sherman's soldiers appeared and began plundering Croly Hill, stealing valuables from them and their servants. They first demanded any whiskey or firearms that were on the premises and then pillaged the house and robbed the servants.

In a journal entry dated March 8, 1865, Bessie wrote of the soldiers:

> They delight in making terrible threats of vengeance and seem to gloat
> over our misery. Yesterday a captain was here who pretended to be all
> kindness and sympathy over the treatment we had received from the
> foragers...but when he began to talk, he seemed almost worse than

any other. He vowed never to take a prisoner, said he would delight in shooting down a rebel prisoner and often did it! My disgust was intense, but I struggled hard to keep cool and succeeded somewhat. He asked, "Do you know what you are fighting for?" I replied, "Existence." He said, "We won't let you have it," with such a grin. I only said, "We'll see." He said, "In four months we'll have the Confederacy on its knees." When I replied, "You must kill every man, woman and child first." He said, "We'll do it, too…I'd rather fight for ten years longer than let the South have her independence." Then, with a chuckle, he exclaimed, "But we'll starve you out, not in one place that we have visited have we left three meals."

In 1870, Bessie married John Julius Pringle and lived with him at White House, his family's plantation in Georgetown District. After the war, the Allstons were financially ruined, and when Bessie's husband died in 1876, she moved back to Chicora Wood, the family's only remaining property, to help her mother manage the place. They struggled to survive, planting rice, and in the early twentieth century, Bessie Pringle began writing under the pen name of Patience Pennington to earn more income. In 1914, a series of her autobiographical letters that had been written for a New York newspaper were collected and published in a single volume entitled *A Woman Rice Planter.* Her book *Chronicles of Chicora Wood*, a memoir about her antebellum girlhood, her family and her experiences during and after the war, was published posthumously in 1921.

The Pringle Family's Experiences in Society Hill

"It Was a Mercy You Were Not Here"

Society Hill, a town located in the northern portion of Darlington County, did not escape the ravages of Sherman's march through the state of South Carolina. The following letter dated March 19, 1865, describes what happened there that month. Rebecca Pringle (later Mrs. Rebecca Frost), who lived near Society Hill, wrote to her brother:

My dear Brewton,

I take advantage of Col Kinloch's going to the army to send you a letter. I suppose you will be anxious to know how we fared with those wretched thieves who visited us in the shape of Yankee soldiers. Our situation being off the main road, was a great benefit to us. Only one party entered the house. They robbed our trunks of what they pleased, searched our drawers, ate our breakfast & then put our silver spoons into their pockets. There was fortunately a captain with them, a creature named Roberts, who comparatively restrained them…The first party visited us on the Saturday after you all left us, & others, some cavalry, came on Monday morning, but happily they did not enter the house—talked insurrection to the negroes, & went off. None of them were insulting to us nor to Papa, tho' they constantly demanded his watch. Our heaviest losses have been at the plantation, & there they were very great.

Hercules hid the horses successfully for two days, but, it is said, one of the negroes betrayed them, & the Yankees sought them out. So they <u>all</u> are now in Yankee hands, like everybody's, except Mr. W. Evans, & Mrs. Williams. They took from Papa's plantation every four footed animal, & destroyed <u>everything</u> but the unground corn for which the negroes pleaded. They robbed the negroes of everything, taking their shoes from their feet, & handkerchiefs from the women's heads. They took off thirteen of Papa's negroes. Scipio was on his way to James, but they captured him. Albert they also took. They took off a large number of negroes from this neighbourhood, & a large number of animals. They have plundered everyone of everything most valuable. Every bottle of Papa's & John's wine is gone. All of our beautiful china & glass that was stored in [Coker's] store is gone and the…staircase & entry carpets were cut up for saddle clothes for their stolen horses. The people in the village had an awful time. The wretches were walking in & out of their houses from sunrise till sunset. It was a most terrible ordeal for all of us, & God knows how we will be able to endure another such trial. It was a mercy you were not here.

The poor people about here told that the men of the neighbourhood were in the swamps, & the Yankees swore vengeance against them—searched the swamps in every direction—captured them <u>all</u>. They afterwards released those who were not in the army. Cousin Alston turned up all right with the [pony] all right too, a week after all the confusion. He had been behind the Yankees at Lynch's Creek. He has gone off to report at Newberry.

We are fearing more raids up here. The Yankees have built the railroad up to Kingstree, we hear. Our servants behaved admirably, & we hid our provisions very successfully, else we should now be starving. We are in a sad plight being cut off from all communication with the outer world. We have no idea where our army is. We hope to have the railroad again established, but we fear it will only bring the Yanks after us. Brother is now here, but leaves in a few days for Spartanburg to join Governor Magrath. Bob leaves shortly for Glenn Springs, where the Gov. has established a camp of instruction for boys of 16.

All united in love.

Ever yours affectionately
Rebecca

Chapter 4

Potter's Raid and Other Operations, April–May 1865

THE INVASION OF SUMTER

"Suddenly Demoniacal Yells Filled the Air"

This town lay in the path of Potter's Raid, an expedition led by Union general E.E. Potter. On April 5, 1865, his forces left the coastal town of Georgetown, South Carolina, and made their way inland across the state, eventually approaching Sumter, their principal object being the destruction of railroads in a region between Florence and Sumter.

Just outside the town, on April 9 (the day of General Robert E. Lee's surrender), a small band of boys, old men and convalescent Confederate soldiers—numbering about 160 in all—attempted to defend Sumter and halt Potter's progress at a place called Dingle's Mill. The Confederates held off more than 2,500 enemy troops for several hours before being overwhelmed.

Two civilians from nearby Manning, South Carolina, had gone down to Dingle's Mill to witness the fight. W.H. Garland, a veteran of the battle, recalled what happened when the two men were accidentally cornered by the enemy: "They tied their handkerchiefs to sticks and said: 'We have not been fighting; we surrender.' But the men of Potter's army replied, 'Damn you, we will surrender you,' and at once shot them."

General E.E. Potter. *Courtesy of the South Carolina Historical Society.*

General Potter's army, which included U.S. Colored Troops, met with no other military resistance and marched into Sumter. Reverend William W. Mood, who wrote an account of Potter's Raid, described what happened next:

> *It would be impossible to describe the alarm and terror, felt by the people of Sumter, as from their windows and piazzas they beheld this army of black soldiers... The officers quartered themselves upon the people of the town... They began at once their work of destruction, and their purpose was to begin with the torch at the Court House; but it was occupied by the sick and wounded, and was used as a hospital. The Jail, the Depot, the large and commodious Rail Road shops, with much expensive machinery, all the public stores, and a vast amount of cotton, were all destroyed...*
>
> *General Potter had strong pickets posted entirely around the town, and the army occupied the town in their camps... They seized the Sumter Watchman [newspaper] office belonging to Gilbert and Darr, and at once published and distributed the "Banner of Freedom." In this the utter uselessness of further resistance by the Confederate States to the U.S.*

Government was set forth, urging the citizens to accept the inevitable. They then destroyed the press and demolished the office.

After dealing with public buildings and the railroad, the soldiers went from house to house and took all the food and valuables they wished to have for themselves.

General Potter's orders also included a directive that the food supplies in his area of operations "should be exhausted." Reverend Mood reported that a surgeon of the Ninth Michigan Regiment asked some ladies from a nearby community if they knew "what their army had been doing on the march?" They replied "only what they had heard—viz: burning all the cotton, destroying all the corn and laying waste the newly planted fields; yes [he said], and even more than that, we have killed everything in our march from a cow to a cat."

In her history of Sumter County, historian Anne King Gregorie related an incident that occurred in Sumter during Potter's Raid. A soldier looting the home of Mrs. McKagen horrified her children by shoving the barrel of his gun into the mouth of their sleeping nurse. The same man asked Mrs. McKagen if any of her family had fought at Dingle's Mill, and the lady told them that her husband had been there and asked if the soldier had seen him. The man laughingly replied that he had found Mr. McKagen lying on the battlefield on his stomach and had stuck his bayonet through him. The soldier was lying to her, but Mrs. McKagen was ill at the time and was so deeply shocked by what he said that she died a few days later.

Elizabeth W. Mullings was a child when Sumter was invaded by Potter's troops. Her father, home on sick furlough, was among the small number of Confederate defenders of Sumter. She recalled:

We stood at the gate watching and soon saw the Confederate soldiers hurrying in. They had fought and lost in the struggle. They quickly sought the hospital building, being safe under the protection of the yellow flag.

While we waited at the gate a soldier turned the corner, coming towards us. He was covered with blood, as he passed he cried out to us: "Do you know a Mrs. L-- here? This is her husband's blood. He is dead on the battlefield. Go tell her."

That evening, at home with her mother, Elizabeth waited for news of her father. Soon her prayers for God's protection were interrupted by terrible noises:

> *Suddenly demoniacal yells filled the air, and our enemies were upon us. I shook and my teeth chattered with fear. A loud knocking at the front door, which was on the street, aroused us. My mother opened it and in walked two Yankee soldiers, who began at once to search the house. One man was drunk, the other sober and civil, and he seemed to be ashamed of his riotous companion. The drunken fellow boasted he was "from Ohio."*
>
> *The gentleman (?) from "Ohio" behaved more like a fiend than a man and his behavior cannot be recorded. At length, his conduct becoming dangerous, my mother felt that she must leave the house at once.*

Elizabeth and her mother got out of the house and found refuge in a hotel doorway for the night. The next morning, they found out that Elizabeth's father was alive and a prisoner of war, and on the following day, he and the other Confederate captives were marched out of Sumter under guard: "The prisoners were sent to Charleston, which city had then been evacuated. My father was very deaf, and for not walking through mud puddles as commanded (he did not hear) was so cruelly beaten in the back with butt ends of guns that until his death, a few years afterwards, he was frequently attacked with frightful hemorrhages."

The Sumter newspaper eventually resumed publication and, in June 1866, printed an account of the Battle of Dingle's Mill and subsequent events in and near Sumter, including the murder of Mr. Robert Rivers Bee, a refugee from Charleston: "We must not omit to speak of the killing of Mr. Bee, which occurred at the hands of United States soldiery, at his residence, about one mile from the town of Sumter... The morning after the enemy visited the residence of Mr. Bee, who was an old man, of 60 years of age, or upwards, his dead body was found in the attic of his house."

Mr. Bee was, in fact, closer to seventy years old, having been born in 1799. His daughter, Julia, left an account of how their home was "filled with Yankee hordes" and that after her father's murder, the Bee family was given a guard for protection—so that no one could enter the house but officers. When the Union forces began leaving the Sumter area, one of these officers, Major George Pope of the Fifty-fourth Massachusetts Volunteers, sent Julia a note of sympathy.

THE OCCUPATION OF CHARLESTON

"No Restraint Is Put Upon the Soldiers"

After Confederate forces evacuated Charleston in February 1865, the place was left defenseless. Most of the residents also evacuated, and their unoccupied houses and other properties were left open to the depredations of the Federal troops who took possession of the city.

On March 1, 1865, Union major general Quincy A. Gillmore, the commander of the Department of the South, sent an official communication to John P. Hatch, the Union general who was in charge of the District of Charleston. Part of his letter noted, "I hear from all sides very discouraging accounts of the state of affairs in Charleston; that no restraint is put upon the soldiers; that they pilfer and rob houses at pleasure, that large quantities of valuable furniture, statuary, mirrors, &c, have mysteriously disappeared."

After General Lee's surrender in April 1865, a large group of Northerners made a trip down the coast on the steamship *Oceanus* to Charleston to hold celebrations and give speeches about the war, slavery, the wickedness of the Southern "aristocracy" and the North's victory. In a book that the passengers of the *Oceanus* published about their visit to Charleston, the authors described their tours of various places in the ruined city, during which they pilfered in public and private buildings, taking valuable papers, books, historical documents and other items. Many of these Northern visitors were members of the congregation of Reverend Henry Ward Beecher of Brooklyn, New York. Even sanctuaries in Charleston were not spared. A church historian recorded that at St. Michael's Episcopal Church, "a large number of visitors, from curiosity, entered, and broke off from the pilasters the gilded and carved ornaments, and took from the front of the pulpit the initials (I.H.S.), which were inlaid in ivory."

Reverend Beecher gave a speech in Charleston proclaiming that the sovereignty of the Federal government over the states had been settled once and for all by the war. Ignoring the fact that the Confederate States of America had its own duly elected and constituted government, he declared under the United States flag:

*Let no man misread the meaning of this unfolding flag! It says,
"GOVERNMENT hath returned hither." It proclaims in the name of
vindicated government, peace and protection to loyalty; humiliations and
pains to traitors. This is the flag of sovereignty. The nation, not the States,
is sovereign. Restored to authority, this flag commands, not supplicates…*

There may be pardon [for the Rebels], *but no concession…The only
condition of submission is, to submit!*

The book recounting the visit of the *Oceanus* passengers also described
an incident that occurred at the time of the evacuation of the city,
before the arrival of Federal troops. There was an explosion at a railroad
depot in Charleston that killed many poor people who had gone there
looking for food, and the authors of *The Trip of the Oceanus* claimed that a
Confederate officer named Pringle had deliberately caused the explosion
and the deaths:

*When the Rebels were forced to evacuate the city, they resolved to
blow up this depot, where the Confederate supplies were stored. The
poor people were told to go there and help themselves. Soon a crowd,
consisting mostly of slaves, was gathered there. Major Pringle had
mined the premises, and was not to be kept from, nor delayed in his
purpose, although so many lives would be destroyed. By some it is
averred that two or three warnings were given. Grant that there were,
does this palliate the deed? Who but a fiend incarnate, would have
given the order to apply the match, until he knew that all the innocent
and helpless were safe from harm? The train was fired, and in an
instant three hundred—according to some authorities four hundred—
human beings were blown into eternity. Not long after this occurrence,
this Pringle was captured by colored troops, belonging to our army,
which insufferable indignity to his royal Carolinian blood, so frenzied
him, as to betray him into the best act of his life…the blowing out of
his own brains with a pistol.*

The explosion at the railroad depot was, in fact, accidental, and the
"fiend incarnate," Major Jacob Motte Alston Pringle, was not even present
in Charleston at the time of the incident. He had been ordered out of the
city the previous week and was in North Carolina when the depot explosion
occurred. Major Pringle did not commit suicide but rather died of natural
causes some twenty years later in 1886.

For a long period after the war, Charleston was under military rule, and some houses and buildings were confiscated for the use of the occupation force and for the Freedmen's Bureau. Most if not all of these properties were eventually restored to their former owners, but their contents were often missing, having been pillaged.

The mother of Major Pringle, Mary Motte Pringle, returned to her house on King Street in Charleston in October 1865. Like almost all South Carolinians, the formerly rich Pringle family was now suffering great economic hardships. In a letter to her daughters dated October 24, 1865, Mary wrote of a relative whose house had been confiscated, as well as the continued pillaging of in the city:

> *Your Uncle is in town, alone, not yet having possession of his house, it being held as a "military necessity." But as a better spirit is dawning upon the minds of our oppressors, it may before very long be restored to its owners, houses, fortunately, not being like chairs, tables, etc. removable to Northern States. A few days since, Bob saw a cart on the wharf taking a handsome dining table to a ship. On the box in which it was encased, was written, "Family relics, from Rebeldom." The more correct notification would have been, "Evidences of Rascality."*

PLUNDER AND TERROR IN ANDERSON

"Carte Blanche in South Carolina"

The people of Anderson, a town in the upstate county of Anderson, considered themselves fortunate that they had been spared the ravages of General Sherman's armies during the war, but to their great dismay, just after peace was declared, a force of about 3,600 Federal troops arrived in their area. This brigade of cavalry troops under the command of General Simeon B. Brown had been sent on a special mission to intercept and arrest Confederate president Jefferson Davis and his party on their journey south.

General Brown's troops entered Anderson suddenly and unexpectedly. The local newspaper described how the alarmed townspeople heard "the wild yell of infuriated men, maddened by liquor and ravenous for plunder."

Some of the U.S. cavalrymen were with the Thirteenth Tennessee Regiment, and one of its historians recorded: "We were now in the Palmetto State, the first to secede from the Union and fire the first shot at the old flag and we did not at that time have many scruples about despoiling the country. We reached Anderson, S.C., May 1st."

In a letter found in the *Official Records of the Union and Confederate Armies,* General William J. Palmer complained to his superior officer about this these soldiers: "The reason I recommend that Brown's and Miller's brigades be immediately recalled to East Tennessee is because their officers for the most part have lost all control over their men. A large number of men and some of the officers devote themselves exclusively to pillaging and destroying property. General Brown seems to have given them carte blanche in South Carolina."

Caroline Ravenel (later Mrs. D.E.H. Smith) lived in Anderson and described her family's experiences in a letter to a friend dated May 18, 1865. While giving music lessons to one of her pupils, she heard gunfire and looked out her window to see a Federal soldier striking a black man with his sword. Soon, other soldiers entered her house and began stealing the family's belongings. They threatened to hang Caroline's elderly grandmother if she did not reveal where valuables had been hidden. The soldiers did not follow through on this threat but instead took Caroline's sixty-two-year-old uncle Henry Winthrop and hanged him from his own bedstead, lifting him up by the neck several times. When the hanging got no results, the soldiers pressed a sword to his chest and also beat his head with a shovel and their fists.

In a letter to a relative dated February 5, 1866, Mr. Winthrop wrote of his ordeal and stated that he had been advised that it would be futile to go to the Federal authorities at the time to obtain any sort of redress for the crimes committed against him and his family. In the same letter, he also mentioned that several other persons in the town had suffered similar fates as his.

Louise A. Vandiver's history of Anderson County records that Federal soldiers hanged Mr. Daniel Brown from a tree while his little daughter watched and that Dr. A.P. Cater was hanged by his thumbs and left that way until his aunts and a servant cut him down. Mr. Silcox, a refugee from Charleston, was another elderly man who was beaten and cruelly treated by the Federal soldiers. The troops also shot and killed a young man attempting to get out of their way as they rode through the streets, as well as vandalized the offices of the local newspaper, the *Anderson Intelligencer.*

CAROLINE GILMAN'S EXPERIENCES IN 1865

"Sherman's Desolation"

Caroline Howard Gilman (1794–1888) and her husband, Reverend Samuel Gilman (1791–1858), held places of esteem in the intellectual and cultural life of Charleston. Born in Boston, Massachusetts, she moved to Charleston in 1819 when her husband was appointed as minister of the Unitarian church on Archdale Street. Mrs. Gilman founded a weekly magazine for children eventually known as the *Southern Rose*. She edited and did most of the writing for her publication from 1832 to 1839 and expanded its audience to adult readers. Her poetry and fiction, including two novels, made her famous in her day, and she became one of the most popular female writers of the first half of the nineteenth century. Her novel *Recollections of a Southern Matron* (1838), set in South Carolina, sympathetically depicted plantation life and southern culture. Though a native of New England, Mrs. Gilman strongly supported the Southern cause once the war began.

Due to the bombardment of Charleston, she and some of her family left the city and rented a house in the upcountry of South Carolina, in Greenville. In an undated letter (likely written in 1864), Mrs. Gilman wrote that her house at 11 Orange Street in Charleston had been "struck by a shell, through the pantry, which entered the cellar without exploding."

In early May 1865, after Lee's surrender, United States troops in pursuit of Confederate president Jefferson Davis descended on Greenville, and Mrs. Gilman wrote an account of it in another letter:

> On the 2ⁿᵈ day of May, Louisa, Carolina, the children & myself, seated ourselves at the dinner table…A sense of calm, if not happiness, was shed over us by the thought that our friends were not in mortal combat, & we had full confidence that the flag of truce would be respected. It seems to me that a Raid is the worst form of war, for its <u>professed</u> object is to attack the defenseless, to pillage women & children, & destroy their homes. What was our horror then to hear a cry from the servants, "The Yankees are coming!"
>
> Presently a negro man in a cart, whipping his horse to a full gallop came tearing along to escape, but in vain, a dozen of the enemy's cavalry came after him & fired…

This photograph is believed to be an image of Mrs. Caroline Howard Gilman. *Courtesy of the South Carolina Historical Society.*

> *Clusters of horsemen passed, & looked, & rode on without a question while in other houses they were searching for arms & horses. One man came on foot, while I was leaning over the [porch] rails, & demanded coffee. I said, I had been without coffee two months. "I hear you have coffee," said he, "and if I find it is so, I'll be damned if don't burn your house down."*
>
> *...the Raiders, about two hundred in number went to Main St. & opened the Commissary stores, robbed the Bank, pillaged every article of clothing from the rooms of the Ladies' Association, & then proceeded to private houses & property.*

In late 1865, Mrs. Gilman left Greenville, observing all along the way as she traveled eastward "Sherman's Desolation. Scarcely a farm house, not an elegant and hospitable plantation residence on the way, all ruin, ruin; and in Columbia the last rays of twilight were on the ruins." At her home in Charleston, she found that all her books, private papers and pictures had been stolen or destroyed, along with many other possessions.

In the early 1870s, Mrs. Gilman moved back to Massachusetts and, in her last years, made her home with a daughter in Washington, D.C., where she died at the age of ninety-four. Her body was returned to Charleston for burial in the Unitarian cemetery, where she shares a grave with her husband. A biographer wrote that Mrs. Gilman considered the war unnecessary and "was never able to reconcile herself to its cruelties."

THE EXPERIENCES OF REVEREND BOYCE

"They Stormed, and Threatened to Burn and Kill"

James Petigru Boyce (1827–1888) was a Charleston-born Baptist minister and educator. After serving as a professor of theology at Furman University, he helped to found a Southern Baptist theological seminary in Greenville, South Carolina, in the late 1850s. Though Boyce opposed secession and disunion—like his namesake, James L. Petigru—after the war began, he remained loyal to his state and the Confederacy.

During the war, Boyce served as a chaplain in the Confederate army and, later, as aide-de-camp to the governor of South Carolina, Andrew G. Magrath, holding the rank of lieutenant colonel. Colonel Boyce was also the acting provost marshal of Columbia and was there at the time of its siege by General Sherman. According to a biography based on his memoirs, Boyce disputed General Sherman's claim that the fires in Columbia began accidentally. His biographer stated:

> *The general* [Sherman] *states in his Memoirs—of course upon information given him—that the burning of Columbia was due to a quantity of cotton piled in one of the streets, and fired by some of Hampton's* [Confederate] *cavalry in retiring at his approach. But Boyce always declared that so far as he could ascertain, then or afterwards, he was the very last Confederate that rode out of Columbia, as the invaders came up the street, and the cotton had not then been fired at all.*

Boyce retreated with the governor and other officials to Charlotte, North Carolina, and soon afterward made his way home, much of the way on foot, to Greenville:

Reverend James Petigru Boyce.

A few weeks later, a small brigade of Union cavalry came across the Blue Ridge, with a view to intercept the retreat of Jefferson Davis and his party through central South Carolina into Georgia. The troops encamped at Greenville, and under pretext of searching for firearms, they searched many houses for jewelry and other valuables. Dr. Boyce's house stood in the edge of town, and the large building and spacious lawn would soon attract their attention, besides the fact that from some source they were informed that the family possessed a large amount of plate and jewelry, including some diamonds. So, after seizing the horses, they proceeded to plunder the entire house, bursting open closets and wardrobes and trunks, and flinging everything about, in the wild search for precious things. Then they held pistols to Dr. Boyce's head, and demanded to know what had become of his wife's diamonds and the other jewelry. He told them quietly that, learning of their approach the day before, he had entrusted all his plate and other valuables to his brother, who had taken them in a wagon and driven away. They asked furiously where his brother had gone; and he answered that he did not know...They stormed, and threatened to burn and kill; but his calm replies at length convinced them, and they left, carrying away [many things].

Many other dwellings in Greenville were plundered in like manner...A party of them learned by inquiry where the bank was; and entering the building, they went promptly to the cellar, tapped the wall till the sound changed, then tore out the bricks, and appropriated a good many thousands in specie which the careful bank president had very secretly walled in, some months before.

In the years after the war, Dr. Boyce struggled personally and professionally, trying to sustain the seminary. In the 1870s, the Southern Baptist seminary was moved to Louisville, Kentucky, and Dr. Boyce moved there with it, continuing his work as a professor and a writer. He died during a trip to France in 1888, and his body was brought home to be buried at Cave Hill Cemetery in Louisville.

John B. Adger's Story

"All Kinds of Things Came Out of Those Pockets"

John Bailey Adger (1810–1899) was a Presbyterian minister. A native of Charleston, he was a missionary to Turkey in the 1830s and later was a professor at the Columbia Theological Seminary. In 1865, he was living at Boscobel Plantation near Pendleton, in Anderson County, South Carolina, and in May of that year, after General Robert E. Lee's surrender, thousands of Federal troops came through the area in pursuit of Jefferson Davis, who was traveling through the state. In his autobiography, Adger recorded that on May 5 "seven or eight" of these Federal soldiers arrived at his plantation:

> *I was lame at the time, and obliged to use a crutch. When they came up, I was out at some distance from the house, but they saw me, and one came over to me. He said, "Are you the owner of this place?...Where are your horses?" I told him I had sent them away so that he might not get hold of them. "Well," he said, "You come up to the house, and we'll take care of you." We went up to the house together, where there were two or three more men...I saw that some of his comrades had gone into the house. One of the party...demanded my watch. I gave it to him but said, "Does your government send you through this country to rob private citizens?" Said he, "Do you suppose I would go riding all about here and not take anything home to my family?"*
>
> *...I followed this man around as well as I could with my crutch, and pretty soon found myself walking with him...down the back steps, where his horse was standing hitched. The man started to mount. As he did so, my back was turned toward him, and I heard his gun go off. Startled at the sound, I turned to look, and saw the man I had been talking to falling head foremost from his saddle, with the blood pouring in a stream from a wound in his throat. The sound of the gun made several others rush to the scene, and two of them raised their guns and were about to shoot.*
>
> *My daughter, Mrs. Mullally, was in the piazza, the only witness to what had happened. She cried out to them, "He shot himself."...I called out, "Don't you see this man is bleeding to death? Come here, some of you, and lift him up." Three of them obeyed. As soon as they raised him it was plain to see that, as he mounted his horse, his gun was discharged,*

Treasure Seekers.

the bullet entering his throat, and coming out at the top of his head. Instantly, they dropped his head, and all three began promptly to empty his numerous pockets which were full of plunder...All kinds of things came out of those pockets. I clapped my hands over their heads, and said, "The hand of God is on you men. Give me back my watch." They seemed to be impressed, and looked from one to the other to see who had taken the watch. It was quietly given back to me...they departed, taking with them their comrade's horse, and all his other belongings, but showing no feeling of concern for him.

Before leaving, the other soldiers told the minister the dying man's name and informed him that he was from Hillsdale, Michigan. When the dead soldier's brother later came to Boscobel to find his body, he expressed his thanks to Reverend Adger for giving the young man a decent burial. The body was later retrieved and taken back to Michigan for reinterment.

Chapter 5

Summing Up Sherman's March through South Carolina

SHERMAN'S BUMMERS

"Deliberate and Systematic Robbery"

In his *Personal Recollections*, published in 1866, Captain George W. Pepper, an officer in Sherman's army, defined a bummer as a forager who on horseback or on foot, went into enemy territory, found horses and wagons, loaded them with food supplies and valuables taken from homes, farms or stores and then returned to the main army with his spoils: "These men were stragglers, not in rear, but in front of the army, and they went before it like a cloud, being often twenty to thirty miles in advance of the head of the column. They would fight anything…With the exception of Columbia alone, every town in South Carolina through which the army passed was first entered by bummers."

The newspaper correspondent David Conyngham described the appearance of these men: "Fancy a ragged man, blackened by the smoke of many a pine-knot fire, mounted on a scraggy mule, without a saddle, with a gun, a knapsack, a butcher knife, and a plug hat, stealing his way through the pine forests far out on the flanks of a column, keen on the scent of rebels, or bacon, or silver spoons, or corn, or anything valuable, and you have him in your mind…Color is no protection from these roughriders."

The Bummer.

Captain Pepper wrote that bummers in addition to the soldiers of the invading main army ravaged civilians, describing a "class of devastations" that were "perpetuated to an extent of which the North has little conception":

> *These may be classified, as first, "deliberate and systematic robbery for the sake of gain." Thousands of soldiers have gathered by violence hundreds of dollars each, some of them thousands, by sheer robbery. When they come to a house where an old man may be found...they assume he has gold and silver hidden, and demand it. If he gives up the treasure cheerfully he escapes personal violence. If he denies the possession of treasure and they...do not believe him they resort to violent means to compel its surrender. With a rope they will hang him until he is nearly gone, then let him down and demand the money— and this is repeated until he or they give up...Again, they prepare the torch, and threaten to burn his house and all it contains, unless the money is forthcoming.*
>
> *This robbery extends to other valuables in addition to money. Plate and silver spoons, silk dresses, elegant articles of the toilet, pistols,*

indeed whatever the soldier can take away and hopes to sell; these are gathered up and carried off to the extent sometimes of loading a wagon at one mansion. "What is done with these?" How many of them finally reach the North "by hook or crook," I will not affirm; some through the soldier's mail, some wrapped up in the baggage of furloughed officers, some passed through the hands of the regular official, having the permit of the government.

A second form of devastation practiced by some of our soldiers, consisted in the "wanton destruction of property which they could not use or carry away." Of this I have the evidence of sight, in some cases, of undoubted testimony in others.

Pianos cut to pieces with axes, elegant sofas broken and the fragments scattered about the grounds, paintings and engravings pierced with bayonets or slashed with swords, rosewood centre-tables, chairs, &c., broken to pieces and burned for fuel in cooking the food taken from the cellar or the meat house—these are the subjects of bitter complaint from hundreds of non-combatants...

This robbery and wanton waste were specially trying to the people, not only because contrary to right and the laws of war, but because it completed their utter and almost hopeless impoverishment. The depth of their losses and present want can hardly be overstated.

According to Benjamin Spicer Stafford of Robertville, South Carolina, some of these "bummers" were not only thieves but also murderers. While Sherman's army was making its way through South Carolina, Stafford and his family were refugees in the Allendale area. Trying to survive by selling tobacco, they entrusted its shipment by wagon with a family servant but would not let him make a trip without some of the Stafford males with him, because they knew that some blacks had been killed by the bummers. Benjamin S. Stafford recalled: "After Sherman's army went through, there were bands of roving bush whackers, Yankee bummers who would not harm [a black man] if he had some white person with him. On the other hand, if he were by himself, they would in most cases simply kill him and take his wagon and tobacco."

WILLIAM GILMORE SIMMS ON SHERMAN'S MARCH

"Sweeping Destruction"

William Gilmore Simms (1806–1870), a prolific novelist, poet, essayist and historian, was South Carolina's foremost author of the nineteenth century. Edgar Allan Poe pronounced him the best novelist the country had produced after James Fenimore Cooper. Following Simms's death, his writings fell into neglect, although recent scholarship has brought about a renewed interest in and appreciation of his works. He enjoyed a national and international reputation in his day, and his historical romances, many set on the southern frontier during the colonial and Revolutionary periods, have been compared to those of Cooper.

William Gilmore Simms was in Columbia during the burning of the city in February 1865 and wrote an account of it based on his own eyewitness observations and experiences and those of many others present. Simms's account was published serially, in March and April 1865, in a newspaper he edited called the *Columbia Phoenix* (recently reprinted for the first time in its entirety as *A City Laid Waste*). Risking arrest, Simms continued to publish articles harshly critical of the Northern occupation forces and their actions, one of which was entitled "Thieving as One of the Fine Arts."

In late 1865, the *Phoenix* articles were revised and published in pamphlet form as *Sack and Destruction of the City of Columbia, S.C.* In one part, Simms recounted the treatment of the civilian population by the soldiers:

> *Ladies were hustled from their chambers—their ornaments plucked from their persons, their bundles from their hands. It was in vain that the mother appealed for the garments of her children. They were torn from her grasp and thrown into the flames. The young girl striving to save a single frock, had it rent to fibres in her grasp. Men and women bearing off their trunks were seized, despoiled, in a moment the trunk burst asunder with the stroke of an axe or gun-butt, the contents laid bare, rifled of all objects of desire, and the residue sacrificed to the fire.*

In the same pamphlet, Simms summarized the "march of the Federals" into South Carolina as "scenes of license, plunder and general conflagration":

No language can describe nor can any catalogue furnish an adequate detail of the wide-spread destruction of homes and property. Granaries were emptied, and where the grain was not carried off, it was strewn to waste under the feet of the cavalry or consigned to the fire which consumed the dwelling. The negroes were robbed equally with the whites of food and clothing. The roads were covered with butchered cattle, hogs, mules and the costliest furniture...

The beautiful homesteads of the parish country, with their wonderful tropical gardens, were ruined; ancient dwellings of black cypress, one hundred years old, which had been reared by the fathers of the republic—men whose names were famous in Revolutionary history— were given to the torch as recklessly as were the rude hovels; choice pictures and works of art, from Europe, select and numerous libraries, objects of peace wholly, were all destroyed. The inhabitants, black no less than white, were left to starve, compelled to feed only upon the garbage to be found in the abandoned camps of the soldiers. The corn scraped up from the spots where the horses fed, has been the only means of life left to thousands lately in affluence.

And thus plundering, and burning, the troops made their way through a portion of Beaufort into Barnwell District, where they pursued the same game. The villages of Buford's Bridge, of Barnwell, Blackville, Graham's, Bamberg, Midway, were more or less destroyed; the inhabitants everywhere left homeless and without food. The horses and mules, all cattle and hogs, whenever fit for service or food, were carried off, and the rest shot. Every implement of the workman or the farmer, tools, plows, hoes, gins, looms, wagons, vehicles, was made to feel the flames.

From Barnwell to Orangeburg and Lexington was the next progress, marked everywhere by the same sweeping destruction.

Simms's own plantation, Woodlands, was also torched in 1865. Five years later, he died in the city of his birth, Charleston.

CONCLUSION

"Sherman's Monuments"

On a visit to South Carolina three months after the war's end, Union general Carl Schurz observed:

> *The track of Sherman's march…looked for many miles like a broad, black streak of ruin and desolation—the fences all gone; lonesome smoke stacks, surrounded by dark heaps of ashes and cinders, marking the spots where human habitation had stood.…No part of the South I then visited had indeed suffered so much from ravages of war as South Carolina—the state which was looked upon by the Northern soldier as the principal instigator of the whole mischief and therefore deserving of special punishment. But even those regions which had but little, or not at all, been touched by military operations were laboring under dire distress.*

Many decades would pass before South Carolina recovered from the devastation and poverty brought about by Sherman's army, and the indignation and bitterness that was kindled in the hearts of its people remained strong for many more. In a letter written to a Charleston newspaper in 1881, Daniel Heyward (1810–1888), a Beaufort District rice planter, expressed the feelings of most of his fellow South Carolinians, and many southerners, on this subject:

> *To the Editor of the News and Courier:*
>
> *I see you are paying some attention to Gen. Sherman's address at Hartford.*
>
> *The General appears quite nervous at the ugly names given him by Mr. [Jefferson] Davis in his book. As he attempts to sneer at Mr. Davis, I, and I alone, probably can give him the opinion of one he won't attempt to shake off with a sneer—Gen. Robert E. Lee.*
>
> *I beg for myself to say that I saw the first soldier of Gen. Sherman's army who crossed the Savannah River, and with him came fire. In a very short time, on the west side of the river, every dwelling, negro cabin, barn, and everything that could burn was on fire. From where I was I could see his fires for forty miles.*

The ruins of Columbia from the front of the capitol.

After leaving Savannah he [Sherman] *went to Beaufort and crossed at Port Royal Ferry into South Carolina proper. I was there again before him on the Combahee River. There again every building, dwelling, negro quarter and barn went down before his torch. And so on did he go in his march of one hundred and fifty miles to Columbia, driving the women and children into the woods and swamps, without cover and without food.*

This did not cease at Columbia, but continued to the extremest verge of the State. Now Gen. Sherman cannot deny this; for there stand "Sherman's monuments" as they are called, the burnt chimneys. Was it less criminal to turn out women and children into the wilderness than to burn Columbia? Gen. Sherman knew, for his scouts were in the city every day for two weeks before he entered, that it was filled with old men, women, wives, young women and children, people who had means enough to get out of his way of his devastating army as it passed along. The mayor came out and surrendered the city in form. He [Sherman] *says that Hampton burned the bridge. He had to make one. Then I leave it to any honorable man on this continent what his conduct should have been as a soldier. He should not have allowed a man of his army to go into that city. He should have built his bridge and gone around the city and continued his march. Women and children are always sacred to brave men. But the General says that this is not war. We admit that it is not with the savage.*

Yes. He sheathed his sword, and with a torch in his right hand he led his 14,000 men into that city, whose very atmosphere was terror. The horrors of that night no one can tell. Old men and women, mothers and children and maidens, in the dead of night, turned into the streets arched with fire and filled with 14,000 soldiers. Is this the nineteenth century?

I never believed this act could be sanctioned by the usages of war, and determined if I ever saw Gen. Lee again to give the opinion of one who everyone must deem the highest authority.

I called on Gen. Lee in Savannah, when on the way to Florida to restore his broken health. After a protracted visit and when about to leave I said: "General, I have a question to ask, of the propriety of which I am doubtful. You will not reply if it is improper." He said: "Ask it, sir, ask it." I asked: "Was Gen. Sherman justified, under the usages of war, in burning as he passed through South Carolina, the homes of our women and children while our men were in the field, fighting him bravely?" His eye flashed as on the battlefield, and half rising from his seat, he said in a voice more emphatic than I ever heard him: "No, sir! No, sir! It was the act of a savage, and not justified by the usages of war."

These were the last words I heard uttered by the great and good Gen. Robert E. Lee.

Very respectfully,

Daniel Heyward

Bibliography

Adger, John B. *My Life and Times.* Richmond, VA: Presbyterian Committee of Publication, 1899.

Bachman, Charles L. *John Bachman.* Charleston, SC: Walker, Evans and Cogswell Company, 1888.

Bigham, John. "The Death of Burrel Hemphill." *Sandlapper*, June 1969.

Broadus, John A. *A Gentleman and a Scholar: A Memoir of James Petigru Boyce.* New York: A.C. Armstrong and Son, 1893.

Bryce, Sarah Henry. *The Personal Experiences of Mrs. Campbell Bryce.* Philadelphia, PA: privately printed, 1899.

Bull, Henry DeSaussure. *The Family of Stephen Bull of Kinghurst Hall, County Warwick, England, and Ashley Hall, South Carolina, 1600–1960.* Georgetown, SC: Winyah Press, 1961.

Burton, E. Milby. *The Siege of Charleston, 1861–1865.* Columbia: University of South Carolina Press, 1970.

Campbell, Jacqueline Glass. *When Sherman Marched North from the Sea: Resistance on the Confederate Home Front.* Chapel Hill: University of North Carolina Press, 2003.

Carroll, James Parsons. *Report of the Committee Appointed to Collect Testimony in Relation to the Destruction of Columbia, S.C., on the 17th of February, 1865.* Columbia, SC: Bryan Printing Company, 1893.

Cauthen, Charles Edward. *South Carolina Goes to War.* Chapel Hill: University of North Carolina Press, 1950.

Charleston City Yearbook. "The Government of the City of Charleston, 1682–1882" (1881): 325–77.

Chesnut, Mary Boykin. *A Diary from Dixie.* Edited by Isabella D. Martin and Myrta Lockett Avary. New York: D. Appleton and Company, 1905.

Cisco, Walter Brian. *Henry Timrod: A Biography.* Madison, NJ: Fairleigh Dickinson University Press, 2004.

———. *War Crimes against Southern Civilians.* Gretna, LA: Pelican Publishing, 2007.

Conrad, August. *The Destruction of Columbia, S.C. A Translation of the German by Wm. H. Pleasants.* Roanoke, VA: Stone Printing and Manufacturing Company, 1902.

Conyngham, David P. *Sherman's March through the South, With Sketches and Incidents of the Campaign.* New York: Sheldon & Company, 1865.

Cook, Harvey T. *Sherman's March Through South Carolina in 1865.* Greenville, SC: privately printed, 1938.

Cote, Richard. *Mary's World.* Mount Pleasant, SC: Corinthian Books, 2001.

Cross, J. Russell. *Historic Ramblins through Berkeley.* Cross, SC: J.R. Cross, 1985.

Davidson, Chalmers G. *The Last Foray: The South Carolina Planters of 1860.* Columbia: University of South Carolina Press, 1971.

Davis, Burke. *Sherman's March.* New York: Vintage Books, 1988.

Davis, Jefferson. *The Rise and Fall of the Confederate Government.* New York: D. Appleton and Company, 1881.

Ford, Arthur P., and Marion Johnstone Ford. *Life in the Confederate Army.* New York: Neale Publishing Company, 1905.

Fraser, Jessie Melville. *Louisa C. McCord.* Columbia: University of South Carolina, 1920.

French, J. Clement. *The Trip of the Steamer Oceanus to Fort Sumter and Charleston, S.C.* Brooklyn, NY: "The Union" Steam Printing House, 1865.

Garland, W.H. "The Battle of Dingles Mill." *Confederate Veteran* 24 (1916): 549.

Gibbes, James G. *Who Burnt Columbia?* Newberry, SC: E.H. Auld Company, 1902.

Glatthaar, Joseph T. *The March to the Sea and Beyond: Sherman's Troops in the Savannah and Carolinas Campaign.* Baton Rouge: Louisiana State University Press, 1985.

Gregorie, Anne King. *The History of Sumter County.* Sumter, SC: Library Board of Sumter County, 1954.

Hayne, Paul H. *The Poems of Henry Timrod.* New York: E.J. Hale & Son, 1873.

Hazen, William B. *A Narrative of Military Service.* Boston: Ticknor and Company, 1885.

Hesseltine, William B., and Larry Gara, eds. "Sherman Burns the Libraries." *South Carolina Historical Magazine* 55 (1954): 137–42.

Hight, John J. *History of the Fifty-Eighth Indiana Volunteer Infantry.* Princeton, NJ: Press of the Clarion, 1895.

Holmes, Emma. *The Diary of Miss Emma Holmes, 1861–1866.* Baton Rouge: Louisiana State University Press, 1979.

Howard, Oliver Otis. *Autobiography of Oliver Otis Howard.* New York: Baker & Taylor Company, 1907.

Huff, Archie Vernon. *Greenville: The History of the City and County in the South Carolina Piedmont.* Columbia: University of South Carolina Press, 1995.

Huger Smith, Daniel E., Alice R. Huger Smith and Arney R. Childs, eds. *Mason Smith Family Letters.* Columbia: University of South Carolina Press, 1950.

Hutson, F.M. *A Brief Historical Sketch of McPhersonville and Her Two Churches.* Charleston, SC: privately printed, 1932.

Irving, John B. *A Day on the Cooper River.* Edited by Louisa Cheves Stoney. Columbia, SC: R.L. Bryan Company, 1969.

Jackson, Oscar L. *The Colonel's Diary.* [Sharon, Pennsylvania?], 1922.

Johnson, John. *The Defense of Charleston Harbor Including Fort Sumter and the Adjacent Islands.* Charleston, SC: Walker, Evans, and Cogswell, 1890.

Kershaw, John. *History of the Parish and Church of St. Michael.* Charleston, SC: Walker, Evans & Cogswell, 1915.

Keys, Thomas Bland. "The Federal Pillage of Anderson, South Carolina: Brown's Raid." *South Carolina Historical Magazine* 76 (1975): 80–86.

Kirkland, Thomas J., and Robert M. Kennedy. *Historic Camden.* Part II, *Nineteenth Century.* Columbia, SC: The State Company, 1926.

Law, John Adger. *Adger-Law Ancestral Notebook.* Spartanburg, SC: Jacobs Graphic Arts Company, 1936.

LeConte, Emma. *When the World Ended: The Diary of Emma LeConte.* Edited by Earl S. Miers. New York: Oxford University Press, 1957.

LeConte, Joseph. *The Autobiography of Joseph LeConte.* New York: D. Appleton and Company, 1903.

Lounsbury, Richard Cecil, ed. *Louisa S. McCord: Poems, Drama, Biography, Letters.* Charlottesville: University Press of Virginia, 1996.

Lowry, Thomas P. *The Story the Soldiers Wouldn't Tell: Sex in the Civil War.* Mechanicsburg, PA: Stackpole Books, 1994.

Macbeth, Malcolm. *An Abstract of a Genealogical Collection.* St. Louis, MO: Nixon-Jones Printing Company, 1907.

Manigault, Gabriel. "The Low Country of South Carolina." *The Land We Love* 2 (November 1866).

Mayo, Lawrence Shaw. *The Winthrop Family in America.* Boston: Massachusetts Historical Society, 1948.

Minnich, Michael Reed. *The Rev. Dr. John Bachman: Audubon's Colaborer. A Paper Read at the Meeting of the Historical Society of Montgomery County,* [Pennsylvania] *at Audubon, Oct. 7, 1903.*

Moore, Frank, ed. *The Rebellion Record: A Diary of American Events.* Vol. 8. New York: D. Van Nostrand, 1865.

Neuffer, Claude Henry, ed. *The Christopher Happoldt Journal: His European Tour with the Rev. John Bachman.* Charleston, SC: Charleston Museum, 1960.

Nichols, George War. *The Story of the Great March, From the Diary of a Staff Officer.* New York: Harper & Brothers, 1865.

O'Connell, Jeremiah Joseph. *Catholicity in the Carolinas and Georgia.* New York: D. & J. Sadlier, [1879].

Our Women in the War: The Lives They Led; The Deaths They Died. Charleston, SC: News and Courier Book Presses, 1885.

Peeples, Robert E.H., ed. "The Memoirs of Benjamin Spicer Stafford." *Transactions of the Huguenot Society* 84 (1979).

Pepper, George. *Personal Recollections of Sherman's Campaign in Georgia and the Carolinas.* Zanesville, OH: Hugh Dunne, 1866.

Phelps, W. Chris. *The Bombardment of Charleston, 1863–1865.* Gretna, LA: Pelican Publishing Company, 2002.

Porcher, Frederick A. "Upper Beat of St. John's, Berkeley: A Memoir." *Transactions of the Huguenot Society* 13 (1906): 31–78.

Porter, Anthony Toomer. *Led On! Step by Step: Scenes from Clerical, Military, Educational, and Plantation Life in the South, 1828–1898.* New York: G.P. Putnam's Sons, 1898.

Ravenel, Henry E. *Ravenel Records.* Dunwoody, GA: N.S. Berg, 1971.

Report of the Committee on the Destruction of Churches in the Diocese of South Carolina During the Late War: Presented to the Protestant Episcopal Convention, May 1868. Charleston, SC: J. Walker, Printer, 1868.

Rivers, Joseph L. *Some South Carolina Families.* Charleston, SC: self-published, 2005.

Saint-Amand, Mary Scott. *A Balcony in Charleston.* Richmond, VA: Garrett and Massie, 1941.

Salley, Marion. *The Writings of Marion Salley.* Orangeburg, SC: Orangeburg County Historical and Genealogical Society, 1970.

Schurz, Carl. *The Reminiscences of Carl Schurz.* New York: McClure Company, 1908.

Scott, Samuel W., and Samuel P. Angel. *History of the Thirteenth Regiment, Tennessee Volunteer Cavalry, U.S.A.* Philadelphia: P.W. Ziegler & Company, 1903.

Simms, William Gilmore. *Sack and Destruction of the City of Columbia, S.C.* Columbia, SC: Power Press of Daily Phoenix, 1865.

South Carolina Genealogies: Articles from the South Carolina Historical (and Genealogical) Magazine. Spartanburg, SC: Reprint Company, 1983. Published in association with the South Carolina Historical Society.

Stoney, Samuel G. *Plantations of the Carolina Low Country.* Charleston, SC: Carolina Art Association, 1989.

Thigpen, Allan D. *The Illustrated Recollections of Potter's Raid, April 5–21, 1865.* Sumter, SC: Gamecock City Printing, 1998.

Transaction of the Illinois State Historical Society 35. "Major Connolly's Letters to His Wife, 1862–1865" (1928): 217–383.

Toole, G.W. *Ninety Years in Aiken County.* N.p.: privately printed, 1958.

United Daughters of the Confederacy, South Carolina Division. *South Carolina Women in the Confederacy.* Columbia, SC: The State Company, 1903–7.

Vandiver, Louise Ayer. *Traditions and History of Anderson County.* N.p; McNaughton & Gunn, 1991.

Walters, John B. *Merchant of Terror: General Sherman and Total War.* New York: Bobbs-Merrill Company, 1973.

War of the Rebellion: The Official Records of the Union and Confederate Armies. Washington, D.C.: Government Printing Office, 1880–1909.

Wells, Edward L. "Who Burnt Columbia? Testimony of a Confederate Cavalryman." *Southern Historical Society Papers* 10 (1882): 109–119.

Whilden, Mary S. *Recollections of the War, 1861–1865.* Columbia, SC: The State Company, 1911.

Wiley, Bell Irvin. *The Life of Billy Yank: The Common Soldier of the Union.* Baton Rouge: Louisiana State University Press, 1991.

Walker, C. Irvine, comp. *The Women of the Southern Confederacy During the War, 1861–5: Original Historic Incidents of Their Heroism, Suffering and Devotion.* Charleston, SC: United Sons of Confederate Veterans, 1905.

Woolson, Constance Fenimore. "Up the Ashley and Cooper." *Harper's New Monthly Magazine* 52 (1875): 1–15.

MANUSCRIPTS AND ARCHIVAL SOURCES

South Caroliniana Library, University of South Carolina:
Daniel H. Trezevant Manuscript Volume, 1865.
Robert Wilson Papers.

South Carolina Historical Society:
Alston-Pringle-Frost Papers.
Armstrong, E.M. "Letter to the Editor."
Augustine T. Smythe Papers.
Barnwell Family Papers.
Caroline H. Gilman Papers.
DeSaussure, Charles A. "The Story of My Life before the War Between the States."

Elizabeth Allston Pringle Papers.

Frederick A. Porcher Family Papers.

Gadsden Allied Family Papers.

John B. Irving Legal Papers.

John Julius Pringle Family Papers.

Logan Family Papers.

Louisa McCord Smythe Papers.

Magrath Family Papers.

Margaret Hall Moffett Adger Papers.

Norris Crossman Diaries.

Sosnowksi Family Papers.

West, Mary Cheves. "Statement in Reference to Burning of Columbia."

Library of Congress, Manuscripts Division:
McCarter Journal, 1860–66.
Louis Manigault Journal, 1861–65.

About the Author

Karen Stokes is an archivist with the South Carolina Historical Society in Charleston, South Carolina, and has published articles on South Carolina history in numerous newspapers and journals. She is the co-editor of *Faith, Valor, and Devotion: The Civil War Letters of William Porcher DuBose* and is currently editing another collection of South Carolina wartime letters for publication in 2013.

Visit us at
www.historypress.net